STRIKE *the* EMPTY

BETH KEPHART

THINK OF MEMOIR AS A BRIDGE,
A STRUT, A SPAN CONNECTING
THE KNOWN AND THE UNKNOWN,
THE DISTANT AND THE NEAR,
THE YOU AND THE ME. THINK OF
MEMOIR AS POLITICS.

The author wishes to thank the editors of *Chicago Tribune, HuffPost, Brevity, Hippocampus Magazine, The Millions, Publishing Perspectives, Creative Nonfiction, Woven Tale Press, Poets' Quarterly,* and *LitHub,* where some of these essays, now slightly adapted, previously appeared. In addition to those directly cited in the text, the author thanks *Chicago Tribune* for publishing reviews of *Riverine, Once I Was Cool,* and *Imagine Wanting Only This,* from which some of the language here is adapted.

TABLE OF CONTENTS

———

MORNING READING IN THE SUN
a memoirist's chant

INTRODUCTION

SECTION ONE: NOTES

SECTION THREE: THE MEMOIRS AND THE MEMOIRISTS

ACKNOWLEDGMENTS

ABOUT JUNCTURE WORKSHOPS

MORNING READING IN THE SUN

—

A MEMOIRIST'S CHANT

She said she'd leave her curtains open
so that she might be seen
in New Orleans.

So that someone passing by on the street below—
the brass flare of a horn in the cradle of his arms,
the powder of a beignet on her tongue,
a pot of jambalaya in her hands,
a rose for the girl who will become the lover—
might, in glancing up,
be expanded by the secret,
by the private exchange of possibilities.

She said this in a room of writers.
She said this to be heard and we heard and we watched
the sun sketching the Tyrian purple in her white hair,
the sun breaking at her shoulders,
the sun sticky as honey.

I'd said, *Remember windows.*
I'd said (quoting Ford), *Drastic coherence.*
I'd said (I would say), *Pablo Neruda.*
And she gave us this,
this passing through,
this glasslessness,

this busy, silent marketplace of two,
which we stretched,
which we rephrased,
which we wanted and uprooted and

took as our own.
All of us did. We do.
Thieving as an act of love.

She vanquished the anonymity of the alone thought,
the isolating lonesomeness of separate people being
separate people.
She read and the sun spilled, the sun poured, the sun reached
our hands, our knees,
our hearts.

She read and we said (to ourselves),
Keep talking,
in this room of the imagined two.

— *Beth Kephart*

INTRODUCTION

———

LESSONS ON THE EMPATHETIC IMAGINATION, I sometimes begin, when I am teaching memoir. Or: *Meander within the space of insufficient evidence.* Or: *Think of what might have been as a prayer.*

The words arise from years of reading memoir, of loving it. An entire wall in my house is dedicated to dog-earred volumes and marginalia and notes to self: *Remember this.* Into five three-inch binders I have stuffed downloaded essays and reviews. Inside plastic storage boxes reside remarkable pages. I seek lessons about life and lessons about form and lessons about all the things I hope I can persuade my students to do—all the things I hope I can remember to do myself:

Untangle.

Decompress.

Don't preach.

Don't bore.

Don't confuse.

Don't be a narcissist.

Don't misplace the verse.

Explain only a little and evoke as much as you can.

Establish agency, generate urgency, prize vulnerability, remain raw. Know the question. Don't force the answer. Make the story bigger than you are by making it more true, and, always, strike the empty—that meaningless phrase, that excessive detail, that tired trope, that obvious epiphany, that unmurdered little darling.

I don't think I'll ever stop teaching memoir precisely because I'll never stop discovering it. In 2016, when my husband and I created Juncture Workshops, an immersive memoir program, we also began to produce a monthly newsletter to celebrate and interrogate the form. With Bill's images as backdrop, I shared thoughts on new and classic memoirs, interviewed some of our finest memoirists, and invited readers to share their own writing or their favorite true stories. At the same time, for publications like *Chicago Tribune*, *LitHub*, *The Millions*, *HuffPost*, *Brevity*, *Poets' Quarterly*, and *Hippocampus Magazine*, I continued to write at greater length about the memoir themes that obsessed me. Over time something unexpected emerged: a collection of insights and provocations that, I hope, shifts the ground for writers, readers, and teachers of the form.

I think of the book you are holding as a house built for memoir. (The paint is still drying. The new floor still creaks.) Into it have walked new and established truth seekers—people with something to say about the lives they've lived, the communities they've found or squandered, the geographies they've translated, the dusty histories they woke to new life, the silent impulses they transformed into plans. I'm there in the midst and mist, hovering near the kitchen, thinking out loud about what it all might mean.

A breeze blows, and a teakettle whistles, and conversations whisk.

There's plenty of room.

Pull up a chair.

NOTES

———

IN THE FIRST FURIOUS DRAFT OF A MEMOIR
WE FORCE OURSELVES FROM THE SHADOWS.
WE FIND, IN THE MESS, IN THE PARADOX,
A PLACE TO REST OUR HEADS.

LIVING ALL THESE OTHER LIVES

——————

ON READING MEMOIR

THE CICADAS are in full orchestra as I write these words. The heat is amber. The air is thick as smoke. You find a cool place on days like these, and read. I have been reading. Penelope Lively. Marion Coutts. Decca Aitkenhead. Sarah Manguso. Alison Bechdel. Hisham Matar. Kim Addonizio. Virginia Woolf. James Baldwin. I have been sitting in one place, on an ink-spangled couch, living all these other lives.

I have been persuaded, in the process (persuaded again, I mean), that memoir is a bridge. That memoir—well-crafted and empathetically received—can heal some wounds, can tame the rhetoric, can become or transcend politics, that it should. I have stood up from the couch and exclaimed. I have stored up passages. I have saved some lines for you.

Penelope Lively, on time (*Dancing Fish and Ammonites*):
It sweeps us along, the ever-rolling stream and all that, nothing to be done about it, but we do have this one majestic, sustaining weapon, this small triumph over time—memory. We know where we have been in time, and not only do we know, but we can go back, revisit. When I was nine, I was on a Palestinian hillside, smelling rosemary (and collecting a wild tortoise, but that is another story). Time itself may be inexorable, indifferent, but we personalize our own little segment: this is where I was, this is what I did.

Kim Addonizio on the writer's life (*Bukowski in a Sundress*):
Whatever the effects on the larger world, writing is a record of one con-

sciousness trying to make sense of it all, or at least to transcribe some of the mysteries. It comes from showing up to the blank page, the empty file with its blinking cursor, and hoping the Muse will honor her end of the bargain and keep the appointment. What do writers do all day? Eventually, we get down to our true work, and keep at it.

Decca Aitkenhead on the truth that is, regardless of how we shape or tell it (*All at Sea*):

My three-year-old son asks me to tell him the story almost every day. "Tell me the story about how Tony died-ed again," he says. And so I do, until he knows the words and can join in, as if it were a well-worn nursery rhyme. He needs to hear the story to make it real for him. But the ritual makes it sound more like Little Red Riding Hood *to me—just another fantastical fairy tale.*

Marion Coutts—no, don't ask me to summarize Coutts. Coutts has devastated me with her raw, brilliant words on widowhood. I don't have the language yet.

Is this an introduction? Is this a tangent? What do we have? The force of memoir in my life. The faith I have in the form. My encouragement, to you, to read.

READING (AND WATCHING) TO WRITE

ON NOT NEEDING A DEGREE TO WRITE MEMOIR

IN GRATITUDE, Jenny Diski's final memoir, takes readers not just toward the last months of her life, but back in time toward Diski's teenage years, when she lived as an almost unwitting, not always welcome guest in the home of Doris Lessing.

Diski had been a troubled kid. Her parents had no answers—and little personal stability. So there Diski was, a smart, rebellious girl on the periphery of grand intelligence, trying to gain some traction. Trying, indeed, to know how opinions get forged.

For weeks I listened intently to the table talk, not daring to join the conversation, not having anything to say, and wondering where and how one acquired opinions.... We left cinemas and theatres, Doris and her friends and me tagging along, and before we were out in the street, they were sharing their judgements of what they'd seen. It was a matter of whether things 'worked', how exactly they had failed or succeeded. Nothing was expected to be perfect, so the conversation was about the way in which things worked and didn't and a judgement was made on the balance. Details of mise en scene *and dialogue were picked out and weighed. On the other hand, Brando was preposterous as Fletcher Christian and wrecked whatever chance there was of it being a good film. How did they know such things? How did they make so many different angles relevant to their final analysis? And how were they so expert and so sure?*

Ultimately, Diski would forge and articulate and defend. But back then, she had to find her way, and she found her way not by enrolling in academia, not by stapling down a thesis, but by listening, by being open to the questions and the cigarette-smoke-laced answers and her own unknowingness.

It took Sallie Tisdale, an utter jewel of an essayist, some ten years and three colleges before she had her undergraduate degree. No one taught her to write, not really. No one, unless you count all the books she read and the pleasures she took from them—holding them, pondering them, sharing them. When, later in life, Tisdale's essays found themselves into textbook anthologies, she was delighted about the money at first. Then she cracked open the books and came face to face with the dogmatics and didactics, all the educational stuff that, it seemed to her, trampled the joy straight out of reading.

From the Tisdale essay "On Being Text":

What none of these (text) books does is celebrate—shout with the fun of Ian Frazier's "Canal Street" or cry at Brooks's "The Mother." They tell the student to make an outline instead of to share a passage with a friend. Critical reading doesn't laugh, doesn't snort in disdain or slam itself shut in frustration. When I recall those midnight coffee-shop huddles, I remember the intensity of the feeling we shared. I remember how much the books mattered. These textbooks don't ponder the way a reader ponders; they ponder the way a textbook ponders, which is ponderous indeed. And I'm afraid that, less than halfway through any of them, the benighted sophomore will be thinking of changing her major to biology.

We read, and we watch, to write memoir. We share what we love and debate what we don't, and it's a human, lived-in exercise. "I don't have what it takes to write memoir," some say, but that can't be true. If we are alive to ourselves and the world around us, we have what we need to begin. We don't need a degree for this. We just need to be willing.

IT'S GOING TO TAKE SOME TIME

ON ETERNAL IMPERFECTION

TEACHER. The word can draw a line in the sand. The students in their circle, receiving. The teacher standing, pacing, leaning forward, saying: *Here is what I know, what I love, what I believe. Here is the accumulated me. Take what you will.*

Later, the teacher who also writes, or sometimes writes, or wishes to write, retreats to her own quiet place, picks up a pen, and becomes a student herself. Here before her lies the blank page. Deep within her tangle a fleeting image, an untamed rhythm, a big idea that can only be addressed one fraction of an iota at a time. Lines streak from her pen, but they're no good. The big idea is a front. Frustration simmers.

Where's a good teacher when she needs one?

On the shelves, she thinks. Right there, within reach.

War & Turpentine, born in memoir and unfolding as novel, is a W.G. Sebald sort of book that has had this teacher-student riveted this past month. The author is Stefan Hertmans. The story is a summoning of a grandfather's life—first from the perspective of Hertmans, then from the imagined perspective of the grandfather, and then again from the point of view of the grandson-writer.

The generative material is the notebooks Hertmans's grandfather left behind, notebooks Hertmans says, that he had not touched for thirty years. When the memoir/novelist finally does read these difficult, gorgeous pages, he must retreat, he says, from the truth. Hertmans writes: "... the painful truth behind any literary work: I felt I had to recover from the authentic story, to let it go, before I could rediscover it in my own way."

War & Turpentine is unassailable. By weaving fiction with memoir, history with photographs, conjecture with facts, it is persuasively human and supremely humane. It inspires the stuck. It un-frustrates the frustrated. It helps us reckon with our own endless journey. It speaks to the questing student in us all.

Here, for example, is Hertmans as he writes of the grandfather who, as a boy, hopes to learn to draw just like this father:

He stuffs the densely scrawled sheets into the bottom of a drawer in his bedroom, beneath his socks and underclothes. The next day, he starts over. Over and over, all winter. Spring comes, the other boys go out walking and swimming, on the first warm spring days they go boating with the girls on the Lys, but he sits at home alone and draws, while everyone else is outside, under the scudding white clouds and the warm air working its magic on the city. He is drawing and making progress, and as he sits there, all alone, he sometimes feels a kind of power inside him, a great deep power that makes him feel like someone, someone who can do what others can't. After his months of effort, it's like reaching the top of a mountain. Don't be naïve, a different voice inside him says, there is no summit, you've barely begun, it's a little clearing on the mountainside, a place to catch your breath, look down, and say, Just look how far we've come already. The thoughts fill him with quiet pride. But when he looks up—in other words, when he thinks of the reproductions in the bookstore he was asked to leave—he knows he has a long, steep road ahead. And even that doesn't scare him anymore.

It doesn't matter how many books we have written, how much we are expected to know, where we sit or stand in any circle. It's going to take some time—and we will never perfectly get there.

FROM POETRY TO PROSE, AND BACK

———

ON THE POETICS OF TRUTH

FOR THE LONGEST STRETCH of my early life, all I had, when it came to words, was poetry. My poems were bad poems. They were mistaken. Sonnets, clichés, mawkish disasters. Who did I think I was? Why did I write these complicated lines? Anyone but me could tell that these poems were just were no good.

Yet I persisted; I believed I had no other choice. I was a kid who felt with plenitude, who walked outside the lines. Weather, music, movement, injustice were my themes. Blindness, sunsets, lonesomeness became my subjects.

Poems became my memoirs.

In the growing-up years, I learned to leave poetry to the poets. I discovered that enjambing a line doesn't always elevate a line. That coloring the prose doesn't always make the telling vivid. I learned that there are words for the things real poets do—accentual-syllabic meter; caesura; feminine rhyme. That there are tools only the well prepared should use.

Still and all, I remain aligned with the poetic impulse—habitually interested in poets who become memoirists and in memoirs written as poems. I am intrigued, say, by *Gabriel: A Poem*, poet Edward Hirsch's book-length elegy for his departed son. It is a work of pristine mourning in which the boy is fully seen for who he was—challenged by tics and relentless recklessness, always the bright splash in the room. This boy will go out during a storm to a party he'd seen advertised. He will not return, nor will he be found, for four terrible days.

Hirsh reports on this loss in aching prose. He reports, meticulously, on his own ache: *He was trouble/But he was our trouble*

Would we have felt Hirsch's loss as acutely as we do had he written prose that filled each page?

We'll never know, perhaps, but we can know what happens when a poet like Brian Turner (who also happens to be a sergeant) does not abandon his poet ways as he writes a prose memoir, *My Life as a Foreign Country*, about his experience in the Iraq War. Turner avoids all temptation to explain. He relies exclusively on the power of evocation. He experiments with many voices, many points of views, the full range of the empathetic imagination. He never wavers from his commitment to the poetical, which we find, right at the start:

I am a drone aircraft plying the darkness above my body, flying over my wife as she sleeps beside me, over the curvature of the earth, over the glens of Antrim and the Dalmatian coastline, the shells of Dubrovnik and Brcko and Mosul arcing in the air beside me, projectiles filled with poems and death and love.

That drone aircraft plying the darkness will veer above seaboards, a grandfather's history, and the trees of the author's own childhood before Turner is done with the image. It will return at the end, as Turner imagines his own death. It will keep his true story suspended inside lush but never mawkish language, within a brilliancy that lights from within and needs no false application of color.

MAKE THEM WHOLE

————

ON THREE-DIMENSIONAL CHARACTERS

IN HIS ESSAY "On the Ethics of Writing about Others," Phillip Lopate observes: "Granted, writing about one's family or intimates can be an aggressive, vindictive act, but it can also be a way of communicating something to loved ones you never could before—a 'gift' of the truth of your feelings."

Those who approach the page simply to expose the sister or to wedge in the final word against the cousin may win the battle but not the war. Art inspired by truth is what we're seeking here—*communication*, as Lopate says, and not the thrill of the vendetta or the pumped-fist "gotcha." There is a craft to literary generosity, and at the heart of that craft lies the writer's capacity to translate real people into fully dimensional characters with voices we can hear, and complex histories we can understand, and countless shadings of grey. Adverbs and adjectives alone can't get the job done. Single anecdotes do not offer proof of another's complicated humanity.

Let me put this another way: Two-dimensional characters are judged characters. They are tropes, stand-ins, overly good or overly bad. Your mother might have said a lot of things that hurt you, but she came from somewhere, she had a history, she was shaped by some things out of her control, she was haunted. What do you know about that haunting? How hard have you tried to understand her? Who was she when she thought she was alone? What evidence of another possible self did she leave behind? What happens when you study her photographs, and what happens when you focus, even briefly, on her own vulnerabilities?

(This isn't just about being kinder. It's about writing better.)

Even when you aren't writing about fraught relationships, it's important to give your reader a rounded view of the other. In *The Soul of an Octopus: A Surprising Exploration into the Wonder of Consciousness*, National Book Award finalist Sy Montgomery isn't just writing of the vast intelligence of these underwater creatures, providing the science, and taking us on her adventures. She is introducing us to other explorers and animal-kingdom lovers—young people, older people, expert people, diving people, people with diagnoses and broken hearts. The idea of compassion becomes as central to Montgomery's story as the beating of the octopus heart.

Montgomery's compassion arises not from sentimental or saccharine prose. It arises from *seeing*. Here she is, introducing us to one of her fellow octopus lovers, a young teen named Anna. Anna is whole here. She is wise. She is neither overdramatized nor underrepresented.

Anna, like all teenagers, feels misunderstood, too. Though a twin, like Christa, Anna is nothing like her athletic, outgoing brother. Extremely smart and forthright, she tells us unabashedly that she is enrolled in a "special" school; that she has Asperger's syndrome, a mild form of autism; that she suffers from migraines, attention deficit disorder, low blood pressure (which once caused her to faint in the anaconda tank), and a tremor; and that she's on various medications. At home, her fish, plus her blue-tongued skink, Laila, help her find peace; but it wasn't until she started volunteering at the aquarium that she felt truly whole....

Now an official volunteer, Anna not only has a digital watch (and knows how to read it), but she knows the common and Latin names for every marine vertebrate and invertebrate in the aquarium. She apologizes that she hasn't memorized all the ones in the Freshwater yet.

"The people here are as different from regular people as an octopus. I feel at home here," Anna says, speaking for all of us, "like I belong."

Speaking for all of us. Anna isn't just the Asperger's syndrome character. She's someone with a blue-tongued skink at home, someone memorizing common Latin names, someone who has something to say. Someone Montgomery took the time to see and offer back to us, in her complexity.

THE BEAUTIFUL STRUGGLE

BY TA-NEHISI COATES

———

ON EXPOSING THE DARK AND THE LIGHT

BETWEEN THE WORLD AND ME, by Ta-Nehisi Coates, has become required reading for every American. I've shared the book with my nephew, Owen. I've taught it in my classes at the University of Pennsylvania. I've read aloud from it to my son.

But before Coates wrote *Between,* he wrote *The Beautiful Struggle,* a drum beat of a memoir about growing up with a Black Panther father in the Age of Crack in the city of Baltimore. Coates's father has big dreams for his children and many methods of instruction. The streets, the gangs are educators, too. Coates himself is smart but distracted, big but not a natural-born fighter, more interested, at least at first, in his comic books than in his father's radical preachings.

But you don't survive those neighborhoods unless you are paying attention, and Coates does. Coates recreates, on these poetic pages, life on the streets, lives in danger:

When they caught us down on Charles Street, they were all that I'd heard. They did not wave banners, flash amulets or secret signs. Still, I could feel their awful name advancing out of the lore. They were remarkable. They sported the Stetsons of Hollis, but with no gold. They were shadow and rangy, like they could three-piece you—jab, uppercut, jab—from a block away. They had no eyes. They shrieked and jeered, urged themselves on, danced wildly, chanted Rock and Roll is here to stay. When Murphy Homes closed in on us, the moon ducked behind its black cloak and Fell's Point dilettantes shuffled in boots.

He reports from a place where I have never lived, a place I have a responsibility to try to understand:

We have read the books you own, the scorecards you keep—done the math and emerged prophetic. We know how we will die—with cousins in double murder suicides, in wars that are mere theory to you, convalescing in hospitals, slowly choked out by angina and cholesterol. We are the walking lowest rung, and all that stands between us and beast, between us and the local zoo, is respect, the respect you take as natural as sugar and shit. We know what we are, that we walk like we are not long for this world, that this world has never longed for us.

But Coates also yields the truth of rare, annealing moments, when his mother rescues him with her faith, when his father listens, when his friends step in, when a teacher cares, when he is given second, third, fourth chances, when the gang that he was sure had come for him and his own did not come as warriors:

They slowed down as they came to us, out of breath, some of them putting hands on their knees. They began laughing and a few of us started to soften our stance. But I stood off to the side, confused and convinced that whatever respect was accorded to the other brothers could never extend to me. One of them approached me—What's up, nigger?—and extended his arm. I tightened in a mix of fear and frustration. I thought of how this would end, just as it began. But then he smiled. I looked down and saw his open hand, universal and at peace. I reached out and gave him a pound.

Coates is taken back by the goodness. So are we, the readers. But that, in the end, is the point: There's darkness out there, plenty of it. But there is also light. We write our memoirs to expose both things. We write, and then we listen.

GETTING TO KNOW YOU

———

ON MEMOIR AS POLITICS

AMONG THE MANY profound and profoundly shattering truths revealed by a recent election season was this one: We still don't know one another. We remain suspicious, isolated, lost inside our own echo chambers. We aren't taking the time that we must take to adequately listen, and have we, truly, ever?

Memoir asks us to excavate our own lives, to study the geologics of self, to speak of exposing, sometimes inglorious truths. We are the subjects of our own memoirs, but are we always the heroes? Should we be?

In "Notes of a Native Son," James Baldwin writes of the death of his father, the riots of Harlem, the ugly injustice of segregation, and the darkness within his own heart. He writes of being denied service in restaurants and of the very particular rage of a very particular evening when he, demanding a meal, was told by a waitress, "as though she had learned it somewhere, 'We don't serve Negroes here.'" Baldwin pretends not to hear. He tempts the waitress to step closer, wants her to "come close enough for me to get her neck between my hands."

But the waitress remains at arms' length. Baldwin cannot reach her. He lifts and hurls a water mug. It shatters. The crowd turns. Baldwin, suddenly awakened from his raging reverie, begins to run. In the aftermath of his pent-up violence, there is this terrible, and truthful, self-reckoning:

I could not get over two facts, both equally difficult for the imagination to grasp, and one was that I could have been murdered. But the other was that I had been ready to commit murder. I saw nothing very clearly but I did see this: that my life, my real life, was in danger, and not from anything other people might do but from the hatred I carried in my own heart.

The day of the election, before all the votes had been cast, I went to a local high school to instruct teachers in the art of teaching memoir, a daunting but welcome proposition. I encouraged the concept of memoir as a way through which we might talk to one another. I spoke of the power of stripping away the seeming glamour of our lives, the myths, so that we might discover our truest selves and our common ground.

Let us write our memoirs side by side, I said. Let us share them in a classroom, in a circle, beneath a tree. Let us ensure that *her* story is as valued as *his* story. Let us give our students the tools, and safe shelter, so that they might truly speak.

Find words for the things you can remember.

Reckon with what you cannot forget.

Make yourself capable of listening to, and receiving, the cracked, hard, lovely stuff of other people's lives.

IT'S ABOUT TIME

ON NOT WRITING CHRONOLOGICALLY

PRETEND YOU ARE TELLING YOUR STORY to a friend at lunchtime, a famous memoirist once advised her legions of fans. What happened, and then what happened. Write your story like that.

But chronology is default. Meaning lives in structure. In the deliberately juxtaposed. The unexpected tangent. The pause, resume, repeat, refer, foreshadow, lately remember, reconsider, now return. The quest to find out. The verse and the song.

Heidi Julavits (*The Folded Clock*) tells the story of her life in a diary in which the pages run off sequence. June 21 is followed by March 3 is followed by July 29 is followed by July 18 is followed by August 2, and she's convincing: This is how life is really lived.

Maggie Nelson (*Bluets*) writes a letter to an ex-lover about her obsession with blue—240 numbered paragraphs that hold every musing, every quote, every memory within the present, as if life could all happen at once, as if it does, ending with: "All right then, let me try to rephrase. When I was alive, I aimed to be a student not of longing, but of light." There it is, her time puzzle for us: When I was alive. But she is alive. She is the person writing.

Paul Lisicky (*The Narrow Door*) divides his time into years, his life into corridors, his thoughts into the criss-cross patterns. It's 2008, it's 2008, it's 2008, and then it is 2010 and Denise, the friend of whom he writes, is six months dead, and Lisicky's marriage to M, the other friend of whom he writes, is about to crumble. Now it is 1983. It is 1946. It is 2009. It is 1984. Lisicky is young, ambitious; he is not even born; he is waiting in a bath house and Denise, *what is this?*, is not dead. You just said she was dead, Lisicky. But now, now, she's not, and we believe again.

Time is seismic. It is a broken circuit, a bypass and a dodge, a final confrontation, a scattering of stones.

We scatter the stones, and then we pick them up. The memories start again. The unquit memoir.

MAKE IT URGENT

———

ON MANAGING TENSES

PAST TENSE IS DISTANCE. It's a Before and After stance.

Present tense is urgency. No one knows what's coming next.

Alexandra Fuller has written three memoirs about her relationship to Rhodesia, where she was a child, and to those who formed her family. She wrote her first memoir, *Don't Let's Go to the Dogs Tonight,* in the wide-eyed present tense. She wrote her third, *Leaving Before the Rains Come,* in the wisdom-seeking past. *Dogs* is full of wonder and wonderful strangeness and a wild optimism. *Rains* is looking back, it is sad, it is about the end of her marriage to the man she falls in love with on the pages of *Dogs.* More than once, Fuller retells stories in *Rains* that she first told in *Dogs.*

There are surprising differences.

Here in *Dogs,* for example, Fuller recounts the tragic drowning of her younger sister, Olivia. In present tense, it sounds like this—the focus placed on the facts as young Alexandra experiences them—the pond, the clothes, the lips, the chill on Alexandra's stomach, the cold shock.

It is almost lunch before anyone notices Olivia is missing.

She is floating facedown in the pond. The ducks are used to her body by now, paddling and waddling around it, throwing back their heads and drinking the water that is full of her last breaths. She is wearing a purple and white vest that Mum has tie-dyed during one of her artistic inspirations to dress us differently from all the rest. When we turn her over, her lips are as violet as her eyes, her cheeks are gray-white. Aunty Rena puts her on the floor in the clinic and pumps duck shit out of her lungs. The green slop is pumped up onto the gray concrete and lies around her head, halolike. My whole happy world spins away from me then—I feel it leave, like something warm and comfortable leaving in hot breath—and a chill settles onto the top of my stomach. Even my skin has gone cold with shock.

When this heartbreaking story is told again in *Rains*, the past-tense focus is guilt and sin. These are words that only distance could yield. The psychological brutality of such a loss, and not its evidentiary particulars:

Losing faith is not the same as losing belief, but it can break the fragile tether between a person and her innocence just the same. On the afternoon of January 9, 1978, when I was home from school for the Christmas holidays, my world as I had known it fell to pieces, and out of the devastation that remained I could never, ever again make anything whole. On that day, my sister Olivia drowned in a neighbor's pond. The sin of omission was mine; my eyes had turned from babysitting, my attention had been captured by the earthly wonders and temptations of a bright and alluring farm grocery store, my trustworthiness had been tested and found to be lacking. "It was one of those things, Bobo," Dad told me, trying to make it better. But I knew it wasn't a thing; it was a fault. Specifically, it was my fault.

Every choice opens doors and limits us. Every choice must be deliberate. Reflective distance? Immediacy? The facts or the feelings?

Choose the tense. You choose the story.

UPSTREAM

BY MARY OLIVER

———

ON AWE

A FEW YEARS AGO, while teaching memoir at Penn, I was blessed with a student who had made his way to the campus from Pakistan. English was still, in so many ways, new to him, but he was determined to write memoir, and I was determined to help him.

Partway through the course, I suggested that he read the poet/essayist Mary Oliver. I hoped that, by studying Oliver's often simple phrasing of very big ideas, he could begin to bridge the language gaps that he was facing.

The exercise succeeded. My student ultimately produced a searing memoir about his Pakistani childhood and the turmoil that had brought him to this country.

The Oliver collection *Upstream* contains some of my very favorite essays from previous collections; the essays bear reading all over again.

But literature, the best of it, does not aim to be literature. It wants and strives, beyond that artifact part of itself, to be a true part of the composite human record—that is, not words but a reality. ("The Bright Eyes of Eleonora: Poe's Dream of Recapturing the Impossible.")

The best use of literature bends not toward the narrow and the absolute but to the extravagant and the possible. Answers are no part of it; rather, it is the opinions, the rhapsodic persuasions, the engrafted logics, the clues that are to the mind of the reader the possible keys to his own self-quarrels, his own predicament. ("Emerson: An Introduction")

Wonder is one of Oliver's specialties—a wonder shorn of sentimentality, a wonder of authenticity. As much as we must respond to the times we live in, we must also remember to live. Wonder empowers us. Wonder breathes through us. Oliver's form of wonder is a cure.

Recently I read the following paragraph, from the *Upstream* essay "Staying Alive," to my students at Penn. We discussed the ways in which Oliver suspends time and leads us into and out of a quiet moment of awe. Then we wrote our own memories of awe.

Here she is, to inspire you.

We are walking along the path, my dog and I, in the blue half-light. My dog, no longer young, steps carefully on the icy path, until he catches the scent of the fox. This morning the fox runs out on the frozen pond, and my dog follows. I stand and watch them. The ice prevents either animal from getting a good toe-grip, so they move with the bighearted and curvaceous motions of running, but in slow motion. All the way across they stay the same distant apart—the fox can go no faster, neither can my long-legged old dog, who will ache from this for a week. The scene is original and pretty as a dream. But I am wide awake. Then the fox vanishes among the yellow weeds on the far side of the pond, and my dog comes back, panting.

CHARACTER STUDIES

———

ON BRINGING OUR CHARACTERS TO LIFE

IN BOTH *Handling the Truth* and *Tell the Truth. Make It Matter.*, I ponder that tricksterish memoir question, How do we turn the people we know (and sometimes love and sometimes don't) into characters on our true-tale pages?

Sure, you might use some photographs to remove the burden of describing that person's petal of a nose and hammer of a chin, though photographs are two-dimensional and time-stamped, taken from angles that are flattering or not, political or casual, but (in any and all cases) curated, chosen, not neutral.

Sure, you might allow a "character" to speak through diaries, letters, email notes, Tweets, but that, too, presents its share of issues. Are letters representative of a whole self? Do emails capture a voice? Do you have a right to the words others sent solely to you?

And isn't there more to a character than how she looked and what he said? What do photographs tell us about how she walked or he smoked or they snored or she wrapped a gift? What do letters convey about the hesitation, or urgency, about that third, mysterious person in the room?

Portraying characters requires memoirists to become adept at many things. Tools are needed. Practice.

As a memoir about the before and after of a terrifying gang rape, Roxane Gay's *Hunger* reflects on shame and the price of secrets. Gay is primarily concerned with the body in her book—hers, mostly, but also the cage that traps the rest of us, too. *Hunger* operates as an explanation and a psychological exploration; it almost entirely sidesteps scenes. One exception concerns a man named Jon, a good man, a good lover about whom Gay slowly loses her wariness:

He looked like every other white guy I saw around town—brown, shaggy hair, a beard, wearing flannel and denim and workboots. "You're always talking shit at the poker table. Do you wanna come hang out with me and my friends?" He pointed toward the distance. "Absolutely not," I told him, wanting him to go away, but he was mighty persistent. I was unsure what he wanted from me, but I knew it couldn't be anything good. Maybe he wanted me to go meet his friends so they could hurt me. Maybe he wanted money. I ran through the possibilities as he kept yammering on. Finally he said he needed to get back to his friends, and I closed my door, unsettled. I couldn't sleep that night, staring at the ceiling, worrying about the strange man who followed me home.

Here, readers are grateful for the specificity—the physical tags, the bits of dialogue, the tension she creates. Too soon, however, Jon is generalized and summarized:

We went to dinner at the nearby Ramada, which had a lousy restaurant but a good bar. His name was Jon. He was a logger. He loved to hunt and fish. He loved Lakers basketball. He had never lived anywhere but Michigan's Upper Peninsula.

As a reader I wanted more—the lights, the smells, the drinks of the Ramada, the tease of conversation, the look in his eye, the noise or silence, the crowd of loneliness, perhaps the time of day. I wanted to spend more time with Gay, seeing just how she sees not only her lived circumstances, but the people in her present world. Generalizations rarely do enough in memoir.

In *You Don't Have to Say You Love Me,* Sherman Alexie combines memory, gossip, accusation, possible forgiveness, many, many tangents, and an absolute profusion of repetition to render his mother and his relationship with her. He indulges in the esoteric, the mythological and the contradicted; he liberally plays with the truth. Alexie talks to his mother when she's not there. He lies to her. He lies about her. He loves her, then he doesn't.

Alexie is, I think, at his best when he sets his own story and ego to the side and empathetically imagines his mother's "desperation and fear." I'm a fan of this passage, for example, in which Alexie stretches out of himself and toward this woman he hopes to memorialize. This is a writer yielding the floor to the most important "other" in his book. We must, like Alexie, yield the floor.

I can only imagine my mother's desperation and fear. She'd wanted to escape. She'd wanted to rescue her kids. But where could she go? Was there a place where she and her kids could be safe? Has there ever been a place in the United States where a poor Native woman and her kids could be truly safe? She had no money. She had no knowledge of family shelters. Did those even exist in the early 1970s? She must have debated her options. She knew that Indian children were often taken from their families for the flimsiest of reasons—as a late twentieth-century continuation of official government assimilation and termination efforts.... She couldn't trust any white officials. She had to go home.

In *Between Them: Remembering My Parents,* Richard Ford assumes the role of a sober family historian as he remembers first his father and then his mother. He is, it seems, most intent on accessing the truth. He writes not to explain or elevate himself, but to hold two people he will never fully apprehend or understand on the page. There are no tallies of winners or losers in Ford's memoir. But there is a straining to see as deeply as one person might see into the life of another.

It doesn't always make for fancy storytelling or exuberant entertainment. It is not shocking. It is not extreme. Instead it is a superlative example of memoiristic compassion. It is hard looking and hard seeing—and it is good, considered writing—so I share it here.

About Ford's father, whose sales job took him far from home:

Memory has pushed him further and further away until I "see" him—in those early days—as a large smiling man standing on the other side of a barrier made of air, looking at me, possibly looking for me, recognizing me as his son but never coming quite close enough for me to touch.

About Ford's mother, shortly after the passing of Ford's dad:

They'd had me and loved me. But to her my father had been everything. So that when he suddenly died, all that had been naturally implicit in her life either vanished or became different and explicit and not very good. And she, who was not truly skilled at life without him—having never had a good life without him—became not very interested in life itself. And in a way that I see now and saw almost as clearly then, she gave up on that part of herself that loved him.

Finally: Nina Riggs's devastatingly beautiful memoir, *The Bright Hour,* written during the final months of her life as a young mother with cancer. There is so much that is right about this book—so much lift and hope even as the diagnosis and treatments grow darker, not just on a few pages, but throughout. We live in the well of Riggs's many losses. We are not trampled by self-pity, dishonesty, or gloss. It is Riggs's ability to very particularly populate her memoir with people we feel we've met that makes her book so riveting, so lasting, and so finally meaningful.

Even the family's new dog, acquired toward the end of Riggs's life, is memorably emblazoned onto the page. Look at what Riggs does here: She builds into the moment with verbs and velocity. She shows us how she first sees this dog in language that is not cliché but also not overly precious or crystallized. She adds a tag of dialogue to bring us two steps closer. And then she lets it be, gives it up. The scene is ours:

When the mystery dog comes out, I am sitting cross-legged on the floor with Benny in my lap. He sniffs us and promptly plops into our pile. Ellie comes over to give him a sniff, wags her tail. He's so shaggy he looks like a Muppet—or like he's wearing footie pajamas made to look like a dog costume. "I don't know," says Tony. "Something about this guy just speaks to me for you all."

Let us live in your well.

FORM BREAKERS

———

ON LEARNING FROM OLIVIA LAING

I'M INTERESTED, as so many of you know by now, in form breakers. The deliberately, meaningfully unexpected.

That's why I've lately been spending time with Olivia Laing's work. Books like *To the River* and *The Lonely City* and *The Trip to Echo Spring*. No one would call these intensely personal books memoir. They are, instead, autobiography melding with biography, philosophy leaking into history, the politics of personal choice set against the tapestry of one mind, one life.

Memoirists can learn from writers like Laing. We can learn, among other things, how to weave the larger world into our private one.

Here, for example, is Laing in *River*. She's been walking alongside the Ouse, where Virginia Woolf drowned in 1941. She has been in and out with her own stories, distracted (in marvelous ways) by literary history and people. She looks up. She finds this deer. Look at what Laing does as she binds herself to this four-legged creature. How Laing teaches us about the deer ... and how the deer teaches us about Laing.

(And ourselves.)

As I rose I saw a deer drinking. She didn't see me as she climbed the bank; then all of a sudden she did. Her hindquarters bunched the way a horse's will, a motion I knew with my own muscles as the prelude to a buck, and then she sprang away. She moved in an oddly rigid, rock-

ing-horse gait, bounding on stiffened legs across the track and into the darkness of the wood. She was neither rare nor extraordinary, that deer. There were thousands like her, as there were millions like me. But there she was, attending to her own path, which, for a moment, intersected mine. She was as unlikely as the iguanodon, and as imprisoned in time. It was a weave we were all caught up in.

Now, in *Lonely*, Laing has shared with us her time (mostly) in New York City, a place where she has spent days and months alone considering loneliness, considering artists shaped by loneliness, considering the things that nonetheless bind us. She has introduced artists Edward Hopper, Andy Warhol, Henry Darger, and David Wojnarowicz. She has watched herself become subsumed by Twitter feeds and false connectedness. She has studied the theater of false intimacy.

Personal. Historical. Big. Small. It has all been necessary. It has all been part and parcel of the story Laing hopes to tell, the story of what happens when art and loneliness intersect:

Loneliness is personal and it is also political. Loneliness is collective; it is a city. As to how to inhabit it, there are no rules and nor is there any need to feel shame, only to remember that the pursuit of individual happiness does not trump or excuse our obligations to each other. We are in this together, this accumulation of scars, this world of objects, this physical and temporary heaven that so often takes on the countenance of hell. What matters is kindness; what matters is solidarity. What matters is staying alert, staying open, because if we know anything from what has gone before us, it is that the time for feeling will not last.

When I talk to my students about building the universal in memoir, I'm talking about the kind of paragraphs Laing builds. I'm talking about looking past yourself toward something else. About returning to the reader with news you would not have had, had you not studied the world as well as you study yourself.

SO THAT YOU MIGHT BREATHE

ON TAKING REFUGE IN TRUE STORIES

THERE'S NO WAY AROUND THIS, no pretending. These are clamorous, uncertain, anxious times. We have to peel away the news, the lurking dangers, the awful injustice, the shifting eyes of the shifting storms in order to, well, keep standing straight or sitting tall.

But when we do, when we momentarily inoculate ourselves by daring to enjoy a ripe peach, say, or slipping into a Netflix fog, we are never fully escaping—and never fully comfortable with the idea of escape.

Loss: it abounds. Future loss: it threatens. The world is calling upon us to be fully aware of its needs and its fractures. And here's the thing: We can't do the work of being there unless we are also there for ourselves.

True stories matter now more than ever. Those who write them exceedingly well teach us about the world, and teach us, too, about how to write the world for ourselves.

Seeking shelter within our many national storms I have been reading. The great novels of this season: *The Ninth Hour* (Alice McDermott), *Midwinter Break* (Bernard MacLaverty), *Little Fires Everywhere* (Celeste Ng), and *Manhattan Beach* (Jennifer Egan). The graphic memoirs I should have read when they first came out: *Stitches* (David Small) and *Rosalie Lightning* (Tom Hart). Two newer memoirs: *An Odyssey* (Daniel Mendelsohn) and *Autumn* (Karl Ove Knausgaard). Books about paintings and painters. The essential *Women Who Read Are Dangerous*, with a foreword by Karen Joy Fowler.

Every time I feel myself unwind into despair, I grab a book and I remember what we're still capable of out here. I recommend every single title up there. To uplift you. To uphold you. To expand this constricting world so that you might breathe.

WHEN THE WRITER WORKS

ON BEING OKAY WITH THE LIFE THAT GETS IN THE WAY

THERE ARE AT LEAST TWO WAYS to approach the writing life.

You can go all in, blinkers on, nothing but reading and writing until the project is done, the contract signed, the book out in the world, and the pressure for Book Two producing all kinds of thick white steam.

Or you can decide that to write you must live and that living takes time and that living may even require you to be not-a-don't-disturb-me-now writer more often than not. You are the mother, father, daughter, son. You are the baker and the cook. You clean the house. You weed the garden. You take the job. The words make their way to you in all the in-betweens.

I am the Type Two writer—working since I was a kid, taking on a panoply of jobs (in the library, at the museum, with the caterer, at the architecture firm, in the pharma company, for the newspaper, at the school). I have always believed that these hours that take me way outside my own messy circle of thoughts are clarifying hours. Perspective-building hours. A chance to remember that hey, in the end, my story is just my story; every story out there counts. Even when writing memoir, especially when writing memoir, putting myself out in the world in non-writerly ways has deepened my grasp on juxtaposition, irony, and truth. I have made it my business to listen to others hope, recast, redefine, transcend their lives. I have continuously learned to bend. I have satisfied my hunger for more, as Jane Hirshfield defines the word:

Why ask art into a life at all, if not to be transformed and enlarged by its presence and mysterious means? Some hunger for more is in us—more range, more depth, more feeling, more associative freedom, more beauty. More perplexity and more friction of interest.

Welcome that perplexity of complexity. It widens your world.

CAN MEMOIR SURVIVE THE TYRANNY OF BUNK?

ON PREVAILING DESPITE THE LIARS AND CHEATS

IN HIS ESSENTIAL BOOK *Bunk: The Rise of Hoaxes, Humbug, Plagiarists, Phonies, Post-Facts, and Fake News*, Kevin Young takes aim at memoir. At inflated, narcissistic memoir, more precisely. At liars who sell their stories as truth, at writers who knowingly deceive. The usual suspects are named and, again, debunked: James Frey, Nasdiij, "Margaret B. Jones," Herman Rosenblat, and others. Young is dismayed. He is disappointed. He is certain that there is real cultural and historical harm inflicted by lying memoirists, and he is right. He writes:

The fake memoir doesn't just stretch plausibility; it traffics in extreme versions of supposed reality because anything less might cause us to stop and second-guess—the reader can't afford to stop and ask whether plausible means "apparently valid" or "giving a deceptive impression of truth." Instead, we are too busy being shocked and awed (or schlocked and awwed). Modern hoaxers obey the magician's mantra: distraction is the better part of any trick's power.

Young recognizes, as we all must, the difference between deliberate lying and unintentional error. He reflects on Oliver Sacks, for example, who wrote movingly in a memoir about the experience of the London Blitz, only to discover, after that book was published, that one of the memories he recounts was borrowed—conveyed to him through a riveting letter that he somehow translated, over time, into his own experience. How could that happen, Sacks wonders. And what does that mean for the rest of us?

Because it does, and will, happen to the rest of us.

Like Young, I've felt betrayed by faux memoir and faux memoirists, sharing my concerns in *Handling the Truth: On the Writing of Memoir* and *Tell the Truth. Make It Matter*. The fact is: Every time I teach, lecture, essay, suggest, and dream up the next issue of *Juncture Notes*, I'm made anxious by the literary form to which I've devoted much of my adult life.

But then I make my way to my bookshelves and cast an appreciating glance across my collection of non-hoaxing, non-lying, non-preening memoirists and memoirs. Helen Macdonald and *H is for Hawk*. Margo Jefferson and *Negroland*. Olivia Laing and *The River*. George Hodgman and *Bettyville*. Nina Riggs and *The Bright Hour*. Paul Lisicky and *The Narrow Door*. Sy Montgomery and *The Good Good Pig*. Abigail Thomas and *A Three Dog Life*. There's a wall of stories that would never show up in Kevin Young's *Bunk*—and there's room for more. True stories written by people who set out to write about what it is to be alive, what it is to want to know, what it is to seek out answers. By writers who feel no need to pretend to be anything more than they are precisely because they know that it's not their one story that makes a difference; it's how that one story binds them to the rest of us.

In a year of endless political mistruth and distrust, I've taken refuge in these elevated memoirs. I've also taken a growing interest in graphic memoirs—stories that don't lean on a pile-up of self-creating adjectives and adverbs and implied exclamation marks to convey the deep truths, the deeper questions.

Take Tom Hart, David Small, and Eleanor Davis, authors of the graphic memoirs *Rosalie Lightning*, *Stitches*, and *You & A Bike & A Road*, respectively. It's the economy of language that I lean toward. The trust each author has in the un-worded.

Rosalie Lightning, about the death of a young daughter, sometimes uses no words at all to convey the emotional devastation of losing a little girl who made the ordinary details of life so exquisite. There are pages that hold but a handful of words: "Three weeks ago—wasn't I a father?" There are images that speak for sadness. There are lines—drawn lines—that declare despair. We don't need to be told how it feels. We can see it.

David Small's *Stitches*, about a boy who is brutally "treated" for a childhood illness and ultimately wakes in a hospital bed missing a vocal cord, brings the reader into the confusion through pane after pane of suggestive image. On page 179, for example, the only words we find within six sketches representing a surgical theater are the doctor's "Good morning, everybody. Here we go again, eh?" and then, from the boy, "I know! Count backwards..." Turn the page and there's a nine-grid spread (a swirl of darkness, a darker darkness, a vague face coming into view, a mouth, an open mouth), only one of which, the last, crests with language, the single word "Ack?" The understatement sears.

And then there's *You & A Bike & A Road*, a record of a bike trip the author takes at a time when, she writes, plainly, unobtrusively: "I was having trouble with wanting to not be alive. But I feel good when I'm bicycling." The sketches are simple. The account is one leg of the journey after the other. The words are "Yesterday it was all shrubby bushes. Today there's tall grass," and "Comstock only has a run-down station, a motel & a bar, but tonight they are announcing the winners of the annual county cat-fishing contest & there's an all-you-can-eat fish fry," and "Turn your head. Horizon. Horizon. Your sovereign body."

No massive claims of superhuman experiences. No wild coincidences. No self-dramatizing theater. Just mesmerizing simplicity. And it is that simplicity that delivers the power punch—that proves that memoir, as a form, still has its place.

A few months ago, *The Long Half-Lives of Love and Trauma*, the third memoir in a trilogy by Helen Epstein (*Children of the Holocaust* and *Where She Came From*), arrived in my mail. I met Epstein years ago, at the 1998 National Book Awards celebration. I read her first two books. This third was written over a seventeen-year period, which begins with Epstein's sense that she's about to write a book about a teenage crush. But that, she discovers, isn't her subject after all. Years of therapy and self-reckoning help Epstein realize that she is not quite through teasing out the truth of a mother who, as a Holocaust survivor, exposed her daughter to debilitating behaviors.

I include Epstein's memoir in this meditation on memoir truths because Epstein commits so thoroughly to finding the truth as she writes. She doesn't entirely trust her own memories, and so she enlists the support of that childhood friend. She's not entirely sure she can trust her instincts about the childhood traumas she endured, and so she searches for facts. The book is as much about the process of making the book as it is about the story itself, and Epstein is meticulous in laying out the challenges she finds herself up against. Her procedural angst mirrors, in some ways, the concerns that Young expresses in *Bunk*:

I'm writing memoir—a hybrid form with no accountability and few rules. How do I know fact from fantasy when I'm the sole source? Some writers say they're writing strictly what they remember; some that they see no clear boundary between fact and fiction; some lie outright and tell the reader; others admit to bending or embroidering on the truth. When truth depends on memory, I have many questions.

We all have many questions. We're all struggling with that word "truth." But memoir will survive the interrogation and the hoaxes so long as we agree that the questions that matter are still tremendously worth pursuing and that the pursuit does not have to be dressed up in sequins to gain our attention or respect.

THE ODD WOMAN AND THE CITY

BY VIVIAN GORNICK

ON COLLAGE AND CONVERSATION

MANY YEARS AGO I joined Chris Offutt, Lorene Carey, and Vivian Gornick on a memoir panel in Philadelphia. A large, overflowing auditorium was ours. We had much to say.

Ever since, I've been intrigued by Gornick. I've taught her helpful *The Situation and the Story* and celebrated it in *Handling the Truth*. I've read the reviews of her later books and followed the controversies she's stirred or quieted. She's got a great mind. She's an incisive writer.

A few days ago, I bought Gornick's *The Odd Woman and the City*, published in 2015 by Farrar, Straus and Giroux. Didn't read the flap copy. Didn't read the blurbs. I was due for some new Gornick, and so I brought this volume home. I sat down. I read.

This thought came first. It's about the Author's Note that greets the reader before any memoir has spooled in: "Reader beware: All names and identifying characteristics have been changed. Certain events have been reordered and some characters and scenes are composites."

Oh, I thought. Oh dear.

But why should I expect anything different? Gornick is, after all, the writer who, after publishing her memoir *Fierce Attachments*, came under fire for her decision to traffic in composite characters and scenes—to create them, and to defend them.

I find writing about truth while deliberately obfuscating truth to be confusing, at best. I want to know, when I'm reading about a character's double chin and bright red scarf and knobby knuckles, that I'm not simply being indulged with fakeries. I'm not a child. If you don't want to tell me vivid specifics about the characters in your memoir, if there is a need to protect those you love or those you hate, then don't tell me their names, don't talk about their knuckles, don't dress them up in mannequin attire. You don't have to make things up about other people for me to maintain my interest in you. You can protect those others elsewise.

(Yes, we need more time on this topic. There are nuances. There are questions. We need more time on this, we spend time on this in Juncture workshops, but now, here, we move on.)

The heart of *Odd Woman*, most charmingly, does not lie in other-people stuff. It lies in the beautifully exercised mind of this writer—in Gornick's deep thinking about connections and friendships, possessions and possessors. It's not the color of another's eyes or the gravel in a voice or the hook in a nose that carries *Odd Woman* forward. It's Gornick's reflections. It's what she has to teach us about who she has been and how she has felt.

The book is a collage. There is a Leonard, a best friend (a composite? a real guy?) who binds the loose narrative—a character whose most important role is to serve as Gornick's foil. There are flashbacks and long city walks and present-day observations and sudden discoveries about the past. No real plot. No big-build suspense. But the pages keep turning themselves. We want to know more about what Gornick thinks.

We want to know more, because, whether we agree or disagree, we suspect we'll learn something about ourselves.

Gornick writes:

There are two categories of friendship: those in which people enliven one another and those in which people must be enlivened to be with one another. In the first category one clears the decks to be together; in the second one looks for an empty space in the schedule.

And:

Good conversation is not a matter of mutuality of interests or class concerns or commonly held ideals, it's a matter of temperament: the thing that makes someone respond instinctively with an appreciative, "I know just what you mean," rather than the argumentative "Whaddaya mean by that?" In the presence of a shared temperament, conversation almost never loses its free, unguarded flow; in its absence, one is always walking on eggshells.

CHANGE THE RHYTHMS

ON LISTENING TO OUR SENTENCES

IN MEMOIRS such as *The World Is a Carpet: Four Seasons in an Afghan Village* and *Walking with Abel: Journeys with the Nomads of the African Savannah*, Anna Badkhen writes of the other from foreign-to-her places. In his seasonal quartet of books—*Autumn, Winter, Spring, Summer*—Knausgaard writes of himself from a room on his property. Still, both writers share a desire, and a knack, for following a sentence to its extreme conclusion—wherever and whatever that is.

They allow themselves to be taught by their own sentences.

What do I mean—taught by their own sentences? And how can we learn from our own? The question is, I think, significant. It forces us to fight against impatience, to work (perhaps) off the computer with a pen or with a pencil, to find truth inside rhythms, to change the rhythms to deepen truths.

Sometimes, on some days, all we have in us—all we should have in us—is one good sentence. So many writers tell me that they write 1,000 words a day, 2,000 words a day—some number of given words, written each day. A regimen. But maybe it would help to think of writing just one good sentence every day. One sentence that taught us something about ourselves and the world because we allowed ourselves to linger over its nouns and verbs, its commas and articles, its question mark or period.

One good sentence doesn't just tell a story. It tells the writer the story. It begs for a next sentence.

MAKE THE WRITING WAIT

ON CREATING ATMOSPHERE

THE BIG STORM HAD COME. The snow had levied down. Massive trees lay like spilled pencils and windows waited for the lights to come back on.

Still, I found myself at a (miraculously open) bookstore, where I was to give a talk with another intrepid writer. I found myself at a bookstore *early*, because I like to be on time and there were driving obstacles and, also, life had lately been getting in the way of my unadulterated reading. It had been a while since I'd bought myself some books.

Among the beauties I carried home is *I Am, I Am, I Am: Seventeen Brushes with Death*, a collection of memoiristic essays by Maggie O'Farrell. A bestseller in London, the title was, I confess, new to me. It shouldn't have been. It's brilliant. Each chapter named for those parts of O'Farrell's body that have been under threat. "Neck." "Lungs." "Spine, Legs, Pelvis, Abdomen, Head." "Cranium." Etcetera.

The pieces prickle with content, of course; O'Farrell has lived a terrifying life. But it's the writing here that matters most. The lull, the lift, the attack, the retreat.

In "Lungs," for example, O'Farrell writes about a near-drowning incident. She jumped off a dock. She couldn't find her way back to air. She was saved. But O'Farrell buffers the dark surround of her near drowning with the precipitating boredom of being a teen. She pays as much attention to all that wasn't happening as to the terrible thing that did.

She gives us waiting.

Some are waiting for bad haircuts to grow out, for their parents to allow them to drive or give them more money or clock their unhappiness, for the boy or girl they like to notice them, for the cassette tape they ordered at the music shop to arrive, for their shoes to wear out so they can be bought new ones, for the bus to arrive, for the phone to ring. They are, all of them, waiting because that is what teenagers who grow up in seaside towns do. They wait. For something to end, for something to begin.

If I were sitting with you, reading this aloud, I'd stop and show you where O'Farrell lodges commas, how she makes the writing itself wait, how she renders, through the accumulation of ordinary things, the repetition of ordinary words, a mood. It's not the words she chooses here that impact us as much as it is her pacing.

In "Neck," O'Farrell yields to brighter language, for brighter language is what is needed between passages about a near rape-murder. Here she writes about her days at work at a lodge—the days before she might have been murdered.

I learn, from the narratives inherent in possessions left strewn around the bedrooms, that people are not always what they seem. The rather sententious, exacting man who insists on a specific table, certain soap, an entirely fat-free milk has a penchant for cloud-soft cashmere socks and exuberantly patterned silk underwear.

Throw-away details? Hardly. To survive the heart-pounding awfulness that is to come, we need those cloud-soft socks.

Maggie O'Farrell must be read.

I feel the same way about Will Dowd, whose book, *Areas of Fog,* likewise came upon me—*surprise!* Will's book is a foray. Into weather. Into history. Into personal revelation, humor, spice. It's a map of days and the map is storm and clouds and sun. It's wherever Will's thoughts take him as the temperature rises and falls. "Writers only ever use the atmosphere for atmosphere," Will asserts, early on, and we can picture the tongue in his cheek. "They never give the weather its literary due.... So here's a place just for the weather: a snow globe without a figurine or monument. Just the weather. And maybe, probably, my reflection in the glass."

Look away from these words toward the sky. Wait for one rocking sentence to come. Give the moment its everything.

THE RECKONING OF COMPLICATED LIVES

ON THE POWER OF SIMPLE TRUTHS

IT WAS TIME TO GO CLEAN. To sort through the stuff of a long and growing-longer life and separate the necessary from the decorative, the idle dream from the essential hope.

This paring down began a few years ago, as I helped my father scour and sell my childhood home. I carried the lessons of that saga into my own tiny house, into the books I chose to read, and into my examination, and appraisal, of the single sentence.

Lately I've been spending time with my father as he recovers from a long season of unwellness. I have been encouraging him to write the story of his life, and he has. Just yesterday standing here, editing his pages, I realized how much I don't know about him, still. How grateful I am for his sentences about broken-down cabins and day trips to Detroit.

Memoir gets knocked around out there. It's a form, and everybody wants to make it pay for something. Make it speculative, make it fiction, make it meta, make it a story told through many distorting lenses, darkly. Or lightly. But working with my dad, and working with the high school students I've lately been *Tell the Truth-ing* with, I am reminded of the power that lives inside the simple truths.

The simple reckoning of always complicated lives.

PICK IT UP. PUT IT DOWN. PICK IT UP AGAIN.

ON FAILING YOUR WAY TOWARD SUCCEEDING

NOT LONG AGO, I launched a new book called *Wild Blues*. I'd been blessed by early reviews. I'd had a local bookstore party. I left the book to live its own life. I knew it had to live beyond me.

Because all published books must finally live beyond their authors. Hammered into print, they're fixed. If they become the subject of talk—good or bad—there is nothing their writers can do.

The only books over which writers still have power are the ones they're writing now.

Here's a story about a book I'm writing now. It began its life as a novel for adults more than four years ago. It began (let me get this right) as an obsession. *I can turn this obsession into a book*, I thought back then. *I can write that elusive adult novel.*

My first draft was experimental, a proud collage.

My second draft nodded to conventions.

My third, fourth, fifth, sixth drafts were a refinement of conventions with a nod to the collage.

My book never sold as an adult novel.

Sure, I was a little sad and not a little discouraged. Sure, I put it aside. But that obsession of mine is an impossible tease, and in time I returned to the book—revoicing, reimagining, replotting the book. *I will write this book as a young-adult novel*, I thought, and I was off. Drafts two.one, two.two, two.three. Drafts two.four and probably two.five and two.six. At the end of it all, two editors expressed interest.

If I could only just ... they said.

And so I just ...

That book never sold as a young-adult novel.

Was I to quit?

Was I to continue?

Was I to doubt my odd but lovely obsession?

Was I to doubt *myself?*

Was I to decide the fate of my story in the immediate aftermath of (another) rejection?

I don't believe any of us should, or can.

Because there are always other ways into a story—novel, memoir, poem, it doesn't matter. Because breaking something down and building it back up is never the quickest route of tunneling into the story's heart.

It is often, however, the *only* route.

Beth Ann Fennelly has a collection of 52 micro-memoirs called *Heating & Cooling*. It's a book built out of small parts, an arrangement of moments, ideas, and anecdotes. Eight total lines on "married love." Three total sentences titled "I Knew a Woman." One single sentence titled "Home Button": "When we snuggle, my left hand finds purchase on his back cyst." An absolutely devastating series of pages called "The Neighbor, the Chickens, and the Flames."

Perhaps the memoir you are writing, the memoir someone has rejected, the memoir you have tossed behind the sweaters on the top shelf, is not a traditional memoir at all, but a collage of well-told moments.

Bring the hammer of the mind to it. Pick up the pieces. Ponder.

Patricia Hampl has a new "memoir" called *The Art of the Wasted Day*. Have you seen it? By no "ordinary" standard is this an "ordinary memoir." The jacket copy introduces it as "a picaresque travelogue of leisure written from a lifelong enchantment with solitude." Montaigne is in here. Gregor Mendel. A pair of Irish ladies from a couple of centuries back. And thoughts on memoir. And thoughts on truth. And indications of the marriage that sustained the author. And the slightest indications of the author's husband's death. It's fairly likely that Hampl did not sit down and write this book cover to cover. It's a book that, any empathetic writer might imagine, Hampl wrestled with.

Just as you must wrestle. Just as you must be willing not just to approach your story from another angle (multiple angles), but to do that work happily.

Do that work with the understanding that often the work is the best and happiest and most controllable part of being a writer.

A MOUNTAIN OF PAGES

ON WRITING ESSAYS

WERE YOU HERE IN MY HOUSE a week or so ago you would have found me on the floor surrounded by paper mountains. Piles built out of the latest draft of my obsession-fueled book, which I'd recently retrieved after months of it lying dormant. I threw away every transition that didn't work, every detail that was stale, every sentence that felt slightly tainted, off, dull, unclear. In the skinny-ness of what was left I imagined an entirely new plot and sharpened characters. I imagined a new voice, a different tone, a different future.

You might think that words and story make a writer. I think a writer is something else. A writer is the person who understands that the best work emerges from the man or woman who agrees to try again.

"The personal essay was born of a smack upside the head," Patricia Hampl writes in *The Art of the Wasted Day*. "Personal essayists are adept at interrogating their own ignorance," Phillip Lopate has said. Annie Dillard defines the essay this way: "The essay can do everything a poem can do, and everything a short story can do—everything but fake it."

And then there's Leslie Jamison: "An essay doesn't simply transcribe the world, it *finds* the world. It makes the world. It remakes the world. It puts a boom box right on the floor and starts playing."

No pressure.

As my Juncture family knows, I walked away from many things a few months ago. I walked toward, and into, time. I'd worked since I was a teen. I worked hours after my son was born. I've worked Thanksgiving mornings and Christmas days. And as fervently as I do believe that our work shapes us, teaches us, finally makes us more capacious writers, I had run out of working steam.

In the hours of now I am greedy for the essay. Greedy to read it. Greedy to write it. Greedy to follow the meander of my own mind so that I might better know myself, which is not the narcissistic impulse you might assume it is. We know ourselves, we strengthen ourselves so that we have more to give to our world.

I've written about my father. I've written about my husband. I've written about a life spent ghosting for others. I have added to my essay collections and pulled old favorites to the floor. I've designed an essay class, and I've been in conversation with essayists.

I've been reminded, throughout it all, of how necessary it always is to shatter the boxes we've been working within. To go out and interrogate all those forms.

EVERYWHERE I LOOK

BY HELEN GARNER

———

ON ELEMENTAL POWERS

I WILL CONFESS to having lost my reading spirit during the final months of 2016. I spent all my available time, it seems, consuming the news, trying to make sense of it, talking long about it. Books I'd ordered were sitting on the radiator shelf, in piles beside the couch, in the shadows of books I, long ago, had actually read. The books came in. They sat.

Finally, following the successful execution of many a holiday meal (if I do say so myself), I snapped off the news and sat on my sinking couch with Helen Garner's collection of essays, *Everywhere I Look*, on my lap. An Australian icon whose "unillusioned eye makes her clarity compulsive," in the words of James Wood in *The New Yorker*, Garner writes about every day life and getting older, small tokens and big gestures, movie stars and writer crushes. She writes about not writing and furniture shopping. She writes, devastatingly, about a teacher she grew, from a distance, to respect. From "Dear Mrs Dunkley":

One day you listed the functions of the adverb. You said, 'An adverb can modify an adjective.' Until that moment I had known only that adverbs modified verbs: they laughed loudly; merrily we roll along. I knew I was supposed to be scratching away with my dip pen, copying the list into my exercise book, but I was so excited by this new idea that I put up my hand and said, 'Mrs Dunkley, how can an adverb modify an adjective?'

You paused, up there in front of the board with the pointer in your hand. My cheeks were just about to start burning when I saw on your face a mysterious thing. It was a tiny, crooked smile. You looked at me for a long moment—a slow, careful, serious look. You looked at me, and, for the first time, I knew that you had seen me.

'Here's an example,' you said, in an almost intimate tone. 'The wind was terribly cold.'

I got it, and you saw me get it. Then your face snapped shut.

This is a simple telling. There is no overreach of metaphor, no adult preening of a childhood scene. We readers are grateful for the absence of literary theatrics. It is this absence, in fact, this simplicity that has made the moment resound. Equally essential, is this memoirly thing: Garner allows her understanding of another to grow fluid with passing time.

As should we.

SHAME? SACRIFICE?

ON MAKING THE CONFESSION

WRITERS OF ESSAY AND MEMOIR are primed for confession—their poor behavior, their narcotic bliss, their scandals and their sacrifice, their abandonment of right causes or generosity. Writers fail and that, in part, is their story. But what about that most common of all writerly failures—the failure to write well or publish well or be happily published? What then? Why is *that* failure sometimes perceived to be the most shameful failure of all? The writer's path is a slippery one. Noisy accolades will be followed by silence. Promises will not be kept. The muse will skip town. Confidence will shatter in the dark of night, and if we speak of this are we compromised? Are we ever actually the writer we hope others think we'll be?

I had been wondering about this when I first set out to write a particular essay during what felt like the end of my writing life. Should I be ashamed of my shame? If I were to speak of how hard it had all become for me—the unfortunate choices that had thrown my "career" off track, the scramble to get a foothold on a shifting market, the hauntingly evasive sentence, the difficulty I was having separating the work I was doing on behalf of others (the blurbs, the praise, the glorifying scripts) from the work I felt I might have been doing for myself—would I lose the respect of my fellow writer-travelers? And if I lost that respect, then what?

But the potential shame of such a confession was outweighed, in my heart, by the relief of writing the truth down. It seemed necessary to speak from this side of rejection and self doubt, to turn that into the story, to knuckle into how the hurt hurt and why. Writing from rock bottom provided a new view—a fresh look at my (non) writing life, a first chance at fixing the many things that were identifiably broken. I'm not pretending that I've healed all wounds; goodness, I am not. I can't read tomorrow better than anybody else, I will make no promises about myself, I can't find the word I was just, this second, looking for.

I'm suggesting that it helped to write the hard things down. To say: *There. This. Now. Me. Bloom and bruise and bloom.*

SHE SAID. THEN HE SAID.

———

ON MAKING IT MORE TRUE

NOT LONG AGO we watched the high-stakes, high-court testimony before the United States Senate Committee on the Judiciary. Two stories. Two attempts to resurrect the past. I sprawled across the family room floor, transfixed.

Perhaps politics will always ultimately dictate who believes who, who *must* believe who, but memoirists are trained by their reading and their work to look for clues. Just days before, at Chanticleer Garden, I worked with eleven exceptional women on the catapults of truth. They wrote of words they love and the room in their minds in which those words live. They wrote of themselves in transition. Then, within the quiet of a greenhouse, they wrote of being on the wrong side of themselves—of not being who they wished to be, or forgetting who they might have been, or setting aside the dreams they'd had. When they were done I asked them to locate the two truest consecutive sentences in their work. I asked them to tell me what made those sentences true.

Later in the afternoon, I shared two passages—one from Casey Gerald's debut memoir, *There Will Be No Miracles Here*, and one from Tara Westover's bestselling *Educated*. There is the searching vulnerability, an I'm-not-quite-sure-ness in Gerald that deeply moves me. There are the absolute declaratives of Westover (and, later in her book, footnotes enumerating the bits of family lore that are differently remembered by family members). Gerald has told his story many times, he tells us, but he may have been telling some of that story wrong. Westover, meanwhile, recounts, unwaveringly, quantifying details and word-by-word conversations from early in her childhood.

Casey Gerald:

Was it a summer night? I believe so. Fall seems too early, since if it had been Thanksgiving break of my freshman year, I would not have dreaded going back to Yale as much as I did or been eager to come back home as I was. It could not have been winter, if only because I don't see a Christmas tree when I recall that night and I know how much those trees meant to my sister. To us both. And since I have told the story of this night many times as being a winter night, then I also have to accept that I have not told the truth. This does not surprise me. I wonder, though, whether I lied because I did not remember or because it was convenient to do so. I don't know. All I know is that it happened.

Tara Westover:

My father was not a tall man but he was able to command a room. He had a presence about him, the solemnity of an oracle. His hands were thick and leathery—the hands of a man who'd been hard at work all his life—and they grasped the Bible firmly.

He read the passage aloud a second time, then a third, then a fourth. With each repetition the pitch of his voice climbed higher. His eyes, which moments before had been swollen with fatigue, were now wide and alert. There was a divine doctrine here, he said. He would inquire of the Lord.

The next morning Dad purged our fridge of milk, yogurt and cheese, and that evening when he came home, his truck was loaded with fifty gallons of honey.

"Isaiah doesn't say which is evil, butter or honey," Dad said, grinning as my brothers lugged the white tubs to the basement. "But if you ask, the Lord will tell you!"

The uncertainty of Gerald's book is a room into which the reader steps. The bold self-confidence of Westover is meant to be received, and not interpreted. Readers will have to decide for themselves which feels most true, most enveloping and persuasive—the not knowing or the knowing, the confession or the report.

GETTING IT WRONG

———

ON NOT INSISTING

THERE ARE SO MANY WAYS TO GET IT WRONG. As a writer. As a person. As a community. Vitriol and hate rush us downstream, toward disaster. Arrogance offers no surprise. Incuriosity is a crime against the heart (and page). Failure to empathize is failure to love.

We see it in our daily lives, in the news, in the books we sometimes read— or begin to read and set aside. It's up to us to ensure that no one finds it in the essays, stories, poems, and books we write. Memoir—especially— requires us to be vulnerable, raw, imperfect. Its authority is inextricably bound to its confessed uncertainty. *It may have.... I wonder if.... But this is only how I remember it....*

Memoirists with a platform can, it seems, forget this. Viewing their life as an object lesson in the rise from this or that, they declare, pronounce, and praise themselves. They deploy research as self-defense, as wall. They seem to suggest that, if they can prove it, it must be true.

Ironically, of course, insisting that something is *true* works in opposition to searching for *the truth*.

You know my preference.

AURA FREE

ON TEACHING MEMOIR

I DON'T KNOW whether you are born with an aura or acquire one along the way, but I arrived and have remained plainly aura-free. I don't have the shoes, the hair, or the height. My nose is an awkward inheritance—not as bad as it might be, but nothing one might choose. My face is so unparticular that it is in fact a different face depending on your angle. I'm not atmosphere. I do not emanate.

I quite simply am.

I teach, then, the only way I know how—up close and personal, no distance here, no lectern between you and me, no clap-clap-all-eyes-on-me, no radiant or radiating buffer. I ask my students at Penn to call me Prof because otherwise we'd all forget who is doing the teaching there.

I come to the writing of your story as if I were writing your story. No glamour in any of this. No aura.

For our launch of Juncture Workshops on a Central Pennsylvania farm, we arrived at the height of an historic drought to a host farm family that was already concerned about every water drop. We settled into cabins that had started out as an old pig sty, say, or a carriage house. Rooms that were big and dark, or small and bright. Three times each day a red bell rang, and we arrived from wherever we were and sat around a big old table (two tables, in fact, pressed together) and ate the meals our host family served. Simple. Flavorful. The goodness of a suffering earth, and its people. The conversations of seekers.

In between, we read, we thought, we wrote, we taught, we debated, we sometimes cried, we shook with laughter. The writers in their seats and me in mine, excerpts at my feet, a fat, white notebook behind me, scribbles on the pages in my lap. My chair was hard and small. In the hours we together sat I don't remember sitting back.

"You teach with your whole body," one of the writers said. Perhaps, I thought. Perhaps.

Over those five days on that parched farm, the writers who had dared to join us both found their voices and transcended them. I neither inflate, nor exaggerate. The walls they'd constructed between themselves and their stories, themselves and their passion for the page came tumbling down. Extraordinary work appeared. When it was almost over, when Friday morning came, we sat together not as new people but as freed people reverberatory with possibility.

I include myself in this.

There are no guarantees in life. Why should there be any guarantees in writing? No truth-seeking, truth-telling teacher of writing can promise any student of writing any more than this: I will listen, I will give, I will yield, I will walk in the rain with you, walk the dusty road near you, wait for you, wait with you. I will push you until you are further than either of us have ever been.

Urgency instead of aura, then. The only way I know to do things.

UPON FURTHER CONSIDERATION

———

*IF YOU ARE WRITING EARTHY SENTENCES
(IF THE WORDS ARE ENTIRELY TANGIBLE, SPECIFIC,
DIRECTED), CUT THEM FREE AND LET THEM FLOAT.
IF ALL YOUR SENTENCES DRIFT (IF THE WORDS ARE
CEREBRAL, ESOTERIC, HEAVY ON STYLE), GET SOME
MUD ON THEM. EITHER WAY, REVERSE YOURSELF.
PERHAPS YOUR STORY LIVES IN THE REVERSAL.*

BEEN THERE, DONE THAT? SEARCHING FOR NEW IN THE LAND OF MEMOIR

FIRST APPEARED IN *CHICAGO TRIBUNE*

SHE SITS IN THE FRONT ROW, leaning toward me, telling a story. There are two sisters, she says, both in their seventies. Each is in possession of a ferociously "true" version of a shared childhood scene. All these decades later, and the sisters still can't agree, still *won't* agree, on the scene—not on its particulars, not on its meaning. One sister has to be right and one sister has to be wrong, but the proof is controvertible.

Imagine the memoirs these two sisters might separately write. Whose would you read? Whose would you finish? How would you know who is telling the truth? Which of the two stories *matter*?

There are lost memories, reconfigured memories, tangled memories, tainted memories, rebuffed memories, and at least a handful of mice at the Rike-MIT Center for Neural Circuit Genetics at the Massachusetts Institute of Technology with scientifically induced false memories, according to a recent *New York Times* story. Given the science, hasn't memoir—a form quilted together with the whisper threads of remembering—become a literary absurdity? How about those who teach and write it? In what cave have *they* been hiding? The I-survived-the-dysfunctional family memoirs, the I-beat-the-odds-on-my-addiction memoirs, the multitonal-grief memoirs: Been there. Done that. Read that. And, besides. Was any of it true?

Move on. Move past. Advance the arts. Stop talking memoir.

Yet here I sit. Beth Kephart—adjunct teacher of memoir at the University of Pennsylvania, writer of five memoirs, author of a river memoir, even, and memoir defender. The cover of my new book on the topic is so self-asserting that it practically glows in the dark. What kind of mission am I on, anyway? Why am I evoking, provoking, and encouraging memoir in the thirteenth year of a new millennium?

Because, I say, to those who ask (and plenty ask), I refuse to give up on this sub-species of literature that can and often does speak directly, and powerfully, to the lives we live. Because I believe that the best of memoir, so often (but not always) written with an "I," is finally, about the "we." Because I believe that our very finest memoirists are philosophers, risk takers, sentence forgers, structural innovators, language shapers. They alert us, calm us, reach toward us. They say (they immaculately imply), *Yes, I have hoped, and yes, I have wanted, and I know that you have, too.*

Many books masquerade as memoir. They wear the label. They proclaim. They operate under the misguided notion that simply telling what happened in the order in which it happened, simply filling in the blanks of memory with the stuff that "might have" been, the words that might have been said, the three-song set that was playing on the radio twenty-two years ago, is art, somehow, and also plenty.

It is not art. It is not plenty. It is not the memoir I'm defending.

I'm defending, for example, Joan Wickersham's *The Suicide Index,* a structurally significant memoir that seeks to understand how the father Wickersham thought she knew could possibly take his own life—a bullet to his head. There is no one answer to this question. In fact, there may not be any satisfying suite of explanations—ever—a point Wickersham asserts both overtly and through her chosen form.

Here, for example, is a brief snapshot of the memoir's first page:

THE SUICIDE INDEX

Suicide:

act of

attempt to imagine 1-4

bare-bones account, 5-6

immediate aftermath, 734

anger about, 35

attitude toward

his, 36-42

mine, 43

In the pages that follow, readers encounter story, research, fiction, assertion, abnegation, and simple declaration of purpose: "I'm writing because I need to understand the story of my family," Wickersham tells us, halfway through. "But I'm also appropriating it, trying to transform it into something I *can* understand. Readers encounter, mostly, a woman—a daughter—yearning to know like we all yearn to know, de-puzzling what will not be de-puzzled, and struggling to abide the mysteries. What is not known drives this narrative far more than what *is* known. The fuel here, in this book of truths, is the wildly imagined and supposed. A poem might be organized like this. So might a novel. But this is memoir, made new and relevant. This is Wickersham with every nothing-but-whatever she can summon up and language in.

Equally fresh, bracing, and humane is a memoir called *When Women Were Birds: Fifty-four Variations on Voice* by a writer from whom we've come to expect form breaks and wing flight, Terry Tempest Williams. This is a memoir organized, loosely, around the lessons Williams finds in her mother's journals—gifts offered to the daughter upon the mother's death. It isn't until the full moon following the passing of Williams' mother that the author dares to seek the journals out.

They were exactly where she said they would be: three shelves of beautiful clothbound books; some floral, some paisley, others in solid colors. The spines of each were perfectly aligned against the lip of the shelves. I opened the first journal. It was empty. I opened the second journal. It was empty. I opened the third. It, too, was empty, as was the fourth, the fifth, the sixth—shelf after shelf after shelf, all my mother's journals were blank.

Twelve blank pages follow this passage. *Twelve.* The reader turns and turns but this is it: a daughter looking for a mother's words and finding only blankness. Finally, Williams begins her search for meaning. She remembers her mother, remembers herself, remembers her world, remembers protest, birds, and love. Each remembering churns. Each remembering changes the conclusion Williams draws. The facts matter far less than the twin conundrums of soul and a survivor's reason.

My Mother's Journals are paper tombstones.

My Mother's Journals are an obsession.

My Mother's Journals are the power of absence.

My Mother's Journals are the power of presence.

There's something brand-new in Williams' memoir. There are lessons she yields about truth—how it survives within shade and shadow, like a forest creature with gimlet eyes that can only be captured (fleetingly) by a patient archeress.

Susanna Kaysen had the same epiphany twenty years ago when she published *Girl, Interrupted,* the story of her institutionalization in the teen-age ward at McLean Hospital. If anyone could claim the right to simply put down what happened, it would have been Kaysen; the details of her incarceration are disturbing, electrifying.

But Kaysen is interested in more than her own saga. She's interested in how documents tell stories and shape memory. She's interested in the misworkings of memory. She's interested in understanding this term *insanity,* and defining it. She's walked the dark forest, too. She's looked into those eyes:

Insanity comes in two basic varieties: slow and fast.

I'm not talking about onset or duration. I mean the quality of the insanity, the day-to-day business of being nuts.

There are a lot of names: depression, catatonia, mania, anxiety, agitation. They don't tell you much.

Girl, Interrupted is a true story knowingly shaped into something that stands apart from its author and her particular travails. It is a memoir that elucidates—not just events and thoughts, but the quavering machinery of the mind. As literature, it suggests new forms, new approaches to telling a story about I. It, like *The Suicide Index* and *When Women Were Birds* and *The Liars' Club* (Mary Karr) and *Just Kids* (Patti Smith) and *The Duke of Deception* (Geoffrey Wolff) and *Let's Take the Long Way Home* (Gail Caldwell) and so many other extraordinary memoirs, makes a case for a category of literature that has lately been too summarily mocked, put down, dismissed. There have been rotten eggs, for sure. But, please. Don't throw out the basket.

And so, returning, which of those sisters' memoirs would you read? Which would you inevitably trust? I'd trust the memoir that the sisters write together—argue over, underscore, half-erase, start over. I'd read the duality memoir they never thought they'd write because that, no doubt, will be the most authentic one. The one that assumes a raw, unexpected, unorthodox, quivering shape because that's what truth looks like, in the end. And that's what it is, to be human.

HOW TO WRITE A MEMOIR
(THE EXPECTATION VIRTUES)

————

FIRST APPEARED IN *HUFFPOST*

I CALL THEM MY SPECTACULARS. Together, we read, we write. We rive our hearts. We leave faux at the door. We expect big things from one another, from the memoirists we read, from the memoirists who may be writing now, from those books of truth in progress.

But what do we mean by that word, expectation?

It's a question I require my University of Pennsylvania Creative Nonfiction students to answer. A conversation we very deliberately have. What do you expect of the writers you read, and what do you expect of yourselves?

This year, again, I have been chastened, made breathless, by the rigor and transparency of my most glorious clan. By Anthony, for example, who declares up front, no segue: "I don't want bullshit."

Continuing:

Sure, metaphors, analogies, and unusual word pairings are permissible, maybe necessary at times, but don't push it. You describe the church as a "raspberry and white candy box with sugarcoated spires and crenellations." Raspberry and white candy box... so the church is some kind of red and white? Might have been easier if you just told me this from the start. But I get it. Everyone and their grandmother have described something as "white and red." So you needed to be creative and clever. And it was! But truthfully, I paused from your story there and fantasized about eating candy and other goodies. And that wasn't your point was it? I assume you wanted to tell me about your life rather than indulge my candy box fantasies? What the hell is a crenellation anyway? Some kind of notch or curvature you say? Fine then, yes, I could see why you used that word there, but I dunno... mind your word choice. If something's pretty, just say so. No need for pulchritude, or enchanting, or captivating, or prepossessing. Pretty does the job nicely. "Sugarcoated spires"... again with the candy metaphor? It's clever, but honestly, now I just need to take a break from reading and grab a Hershey's bar.

He's got good teeth, our Anthony, a wholesome smile. He has little patience for the self-conscious redirect, the aggrandizing contortion. Give him the scoop. Leave the sprinkles at home. Tell him the un-spangled truth.

Or, as Heather says, leave the "boasting, superfluous language" aside, the "lack of humility." "Give us the quirks, the dirt, the neurotic tics, the unspoken," and do it in "wonderfully expressive plain English."

Go deep. Go real. Go unvarnished. Listen, please, to Synae:

I want to experience your story the way you experienced it, to love desper-ately, hate passionately, and persistently search for answers to the ques-tions that you've encountered and continue to face. I want you to write as if by writing you are leaving tiny fragments of your journey in this life for an older, more senile you, to experience and relive. These fragments must therefore be vivid, though not so full of explanation they render a story of your life that you've already left and have no desire to return to. They must be snippets of the ordinary so remarkable that they succeed in evoking the same sentiment they once evoked in a younger, more fragile, version of you, but for a different reason. A reason that is full of experi-ence and wisdom in understanding now, what would have made your tiny fragment less sorrowful or more hopeful at the time.

Inflated will never do. The look-at-me-and-only-at-me epic. Don't try to tell us everything, our David says. Just "isolate one lovely shell, a conch of wisdom."

I liken this to a student doing long division. In the margins we see the legwork, the scribbled arithmetic and the toiling down and down, until we arrive at the answer – the universalism that extends outward from the work. And, in this respect, the author's life may be mundane if such a thing exists (it does not) or unbelievable, for it is not the events them-selves, riveting as some of the scenes may be that engage me. It is the author's dissection of them that comes of the prevailing will to be under-stood by others and to understand himself.

If Kasey exhorts the memoirist to "take me away, design my mind, make me fall in love, make my heart race, challenge me," and Stephanie requires brave exploration, the writing of stories that "feel as though they're about something bigger than themselves," and Anita asks the memoirist to inspire, to surprise, to craft and yield a "distinct voice," and Devin values, above all else "candor and admission for things that go wrong because that is how they actually happened or that is the natu-ral consequence of an imagined situation," then Silvia asks the memoir-ist to stand up straight and be a thinker:

Tell me the why and tell me the how of the world around me that I've not the time, energy, or skill to notice. Put into words the rhythm of my heartbeat—or the things my heart beats for. Make me visualize dimen-sions that are all too often forgotten, and revive in them the urgency with which we must learn from them. Talk about tendons; talk about sidewalks—use them as analogies to illustrate my dreams, explain my past, conceptualize my desires.

And if you can both think deep and poeticize, go ahead, Dani says, with a wink at Anthony, and take the chance. Go ahead, with care and craft. "I read to find disorientation, get drunk off a simile. I expect no less than a beautiful hangover. I expect nothing less than synesthesia." And while Elly's not calling for synesthesia in every memoir she reads, she is calling for memoirists who possess that "powerful ability of being comfortable with their own voice."

That comfort—it takes many shapes. But we know it when we see it. Please (again). Be yourself on the page. Do not be afraid of your broken pieces. Says Nina:

I don't want to open a book and see that every sentence is flawlessly crafted, no chapter lingers on for too long, all plot lines are wrapped up in a pretty little bow and handed to me on a silver platter. Perfection like that is too easy. I want writers who communicate complexity through flaws, within failures.

And then, and then almost finally (for there is no finally, there is just the bar being magnificently raised), write what we can love, write something that lasts, write from within a Big Hope, which is to say, write for all of us.

This, indeed, is what Hannah asks. This is incumbent upon you:

Writers: take me on journeys that mean something. Write things that I'll look up years later because I loved them. Write a book I could bring to an island and refuse to tire of. Write a book that I can reread thirty, forty, fifty times. Write a book I'll loan to all of my friends. Write a book that makes me laugh, or cry, or both. Write a book that makes me want to visit your house for a cup of tea to talk about it. Write a book that leaves witty inside jokes like treasures within the pages. Write a book that will make me feel that I am a different person than the one who began reading by the time I am at the end.

Leave something beautiful inside my head.

AND THERE'S YOUR MOTHER, CALLING OUT TO YOU: IN PURSUIT OF MEMORY

FIRST APPEARED IN *BREVITY*

BEFORE I SAT DOWN to write this essay, I stepped outside and took a walk. Always a walk before I write.

I hadn't counted on the winds, or the pewter-colored clouds massing overhead and crowding out the sun. The first drops of rain were a sweet release from heat. After that, it was an all-out storm—the rain falling white and thick. I stood beneath the fringe of two tall evergreens to wait the wild weather out.

Between my feet and the asphalt edge of the street a river began to run. Five inches high, six inches wide, carrying leaves, broken twigs, uprooted fists of grass, something silver and manmade. The sudden river took me back to my childhood and the creek that ran behind my neighbors' houses. To dark shade and cool moist; bare feet in chocolate muck; to water striders and tadpoles, my mother calling my brother, sister and me home.

Memoir is, among many other things, about *what* we remember; it is also about *how* memory is returned to us. About where we go to access the past and what we do when it floods straight through us. Having written five memoirs, read hundreds more, and taught memoir to students through the years, I have come to the conclusion that those who write most knowingly about the past are those who understand what it is to stay open to the tug of long ago. Proust had it right, in *Remembrance of Things Past*. We all have our "petite madeleines," our "exquisite pleasures" that tug us toward our story-able *then*.

"I don't have a good-enough memory to write a 2,000-word memoir," my students will sometimes say. "I don't have enough to go on." And so we sit together and figure it out. What keys? Which doors? Where are the memories hiding? We talk about the difference between provoking and evoking. We find their memory portals and their memory language.

A student writing about the early death of her brother located her story in photographs—of her brother's childhood room, of her brother's childhood toys, of some of her brother's old clothes.

Another student found his memoir in music and concert stubs—the auditory and the tactile. Another found her past in interviews—the memories of others provoking memories in herself. The smell and heat of fresh bagels prompted one student; for another, memory lay in the art she'd produced as a teen in China and, later, in Canada. A startlingly powerful thumbprint portrait. A brightly decorated chair. A memoir.

I can't remember, we insist. And then we do.

I've found my own past in a box of letters. (*That's* what he said.) In a book of childhood watercolors. (*That's* how I saw.) In the raw burst of urgent, nearly forgotten poems. (*That's* how I was feeling.) In the face of a cereal box. (*Those* were the words that my young son read.) Along the sea at low tide. (*Here* is where my uncle was happiest.) On a crayon wrapper. (*This* is the color he said his skin was.) In a karaoke song. (Now that I remember the song, I remember the day, I remember how we laughed afterward.)

I've found it in a very specific sunrise pink (they saved me that day), and in the circus sounds of those horseshow grounds (heralding the taste of lemons), and on the banks of a pond in winter (it was like *this* on the day I first began to skate). I've found my past when I've gone outside to watch a cardinal peck at the berries on a bush. I've found it by driving to the mountains and staying at the inn where my family stayed when I was a child.

Often memories just find us; it's true. They besiege us, blindside us, shadow us, tag us, populate our dreams. And while writing memoir is certainly a far more sophisticated enterprise than simply writing our memories down, it can be helpful (when not overwhelming) to have so much raw memory at hand.

But when we come up empty, when the past is a blank, when we are not sure, when we are bereft of *then*, when it could have been *this* or it could have been *that*, when we are fuzzy, the gig is not up. We are not done in. We will not get an "incomplete" on Prof Kephart's memoir project. There are photographs, songs, artifacts, letters, landscapes to return to, a book of watercolors.

And always—always—there is weather, powerful as any madeleine. There is a quality of sun that will take us back—stand there; feel it; let it. There is a kind of breeze that will blow, a breeze you've felt before—remember when and remember how and remember why it mattered. There is the taste of snow on your tongue; you've tasted that before: Where were you? Who were you?

And then there's the storm that you didn't see coming and the evergreens that don't save you and the sudden river that runs. You can slosh home and strip away your damp clothes and turn on the warm shower and feel nothing. Or you can stand at the river—slightly cold and utterly saturated—and watch the broken twigs course down. You can stand and watch and your mother's suddenly there—calling out for you.

THE ART OF THE SUPPOSE

———

FIRST APPEARED IN *HIPPOCAMPUS MAGAZINE*

There's no truth like the real truth, the saying goes, but where, in this world, is that truth? Perhaps it lives—in part—in the art of the suppose.

In *Notes of a Native Son*, James Baldwin writes movingly of his father's death and the vacuum his father left behind. Baldwin was, he'd said, been "inclined to be contemptuous of my father, for the conditions of his life, for the conditions of our lives. When his life had ended I began to wonder about that life and also, in a new way, to be apprehensive about my own. I had not known my father very well..... When he was dead I realized that I had hardly ever spoken to him. When he had been dead a long time I began to wish I had."

Baldwin must imagine his father back into life. He must reinvigorate him with shards of remembered images and moments. He must suppose, and he must suppose out loud. He must allow us, his readers, to discover him in the act of reconstruction. Writes Baldwin, "He was, I think, very handsome. I gather this from photographs and from my own memories of him, dressed in his Sunday best and on his way to preach a sermon somewhere, when I was little. Handsome, proud, and ingrown, 'like a toenail,' somebody said."

He was *I think.*

I gather this from.

Like somebody said.

Baldwin's facts aren't immediately on hand; they are elusive. Baldwin must go searching. He must rely on what he does remember, what the photographs teach, what others said. He must research his own father in order to have any hope of finding the truth of him. The truth *about* him.

In *Notes of a Native Son*, Baldwin is not inventing his father. He is, as I have said, imagining him. He is turning a lost-ness into a found-ness. He is transforming the dead into the living. It is alchemical.

There is, Patricia Hampl has said, a "truth of noticing." The truth eludes us when (and because) we do not notice well enough, deeply enough, with perfect discipline or honorable equanimity. We don't remember the year, the name, the socks he wore. We don't remember the words he used to say *I love you,* though we're sure he would never say that, not precisely. We don't remember why we ran so fast or why we stopped fighting or whether the bird that sang was a mourning dove or a finch. Seems that we should remember that. They're very different birds.

We can't take life in or write it down in its rich detail or its 360-degree complexity—ever. Right this very second you are ignoring, forgetting, mish-mashing—in this real-time, in this room, beneath these lights, in your seat, reading this, also listening to a thought in your head, also distracted by your hunger for chocolate. How much of this instant have you perceived? How much of it will you remember later?

The truth is elusive—as it is happening and as it yearns to be recalled. The truth is incomplete, rubbed off, rubbed down, permeated, bullet-holed, twisted, more than the facts themselves, but reliant, at least in part, on the facts. Still, we are desperate for it. We won't stop trying. And here's the interesting thing: We are most trusted as memoirists when we acknowledge our difficulty, our trying, our perilous attempts at knowing. We are most close to the truth when we admit how nearly impossible the truth so often is.

"Somewhere deep in my childhood, my father is coming off the road on a Friday night," Richard Ford writes in *Between Them*. "He is a traveling salesman. It is 1951 or '52. He's carrying with him lumpy, white butcher-paper packages full of boiled shrimp or tamales or oysters-by-the-pint he's brought up from Louisiana. The shrimp and tamales steam up hot and damp off the slick papers when he opens them out. Lights in our small duplex on Congress Street in Jackson are switched on bright. My father, Parker Ford, is a large man—soft, heavy-seeming, smiling widely as if he knew a funny joke. He is excited to be home."

Did you hear that? Did you hear how Ford halved the distance between what he knows for sure—Congress Street, Jackson, the fact of the duplex, the name of his father—and what he senses? *Somewhere deep in my childhood,* he begins. Packages of boiled shrimp OR tamales OR oysters-by-the-pint. Heavy-*seeming*. Ford has gathered the details of what he knows for certain and plied them into a moment of fairytale expanse. It's not that it happened just like this in a certain hour on a certain day in a certain month. It's that it *could have* happened. It's that it probably did. It's that the essence of Parker Ford is the truest stuff of Parker Ford. It's that Richard Ford does not pretend to know anymore than he actually does.

James Baldwin. Richard Ford. Giants of literature who are not afraid to negotiate the maybe and the suppose. Casey Gerald's *There Will Be No Miracles Here* is an exemplar of the art of the suppose, and I encourage you to look for it. And if you need one more example, listen to Patti Smith, the rocker and lyric memoirist. She's not afraid to say what she doesn't know for certain either, nor is she afraid to name what she is, in fact, certain of.

From *Just Kids*: "When I was very young, my mother took me for walks in Humboldt Park, along the edge of the Prairie River. I have vague memories, like impressions on glass plates, of an old boathouse, a circular band shell, an arched stone bridge. The narrows of the river emptied into a wide lagoon and I saw upon its surface a singular miracle. A long curving neck rose from a dress of white plumage./ *Swan*, my mother said, sensing my excitement. It pattered the bright water, flapping its great wings, and lifted into the sky."

The truth is elusive, but don't let that defeat you. Let truth's elusivity galvanize you toward the deep dive for the facts, the shimmery details, the startle of a color red or a wind storm or a mother's muffins. Get the details you need from photos, get them from songs, get them from conversations with those you love, get them from maps, get them from phone books, get them from diaries, get them from text messages, get them from the day you set aside to dream.

Let truth's elusivity galvanize you toward pure and pure-hearted research, then let it lead you toward the self-forgiving act of locating the essence that lives between all the facts you cannot find.

Announce the maybe. Announce the suppose. You won't be telling the truth otherwise.

THE SIGNIFYING LIFE: IN PRAISE OF THE OUTWARD-LOOKING MEMOIR

FIRST APPEARED IN *THE MILLIONS*

WHY, IN THE END, do we read memoir? What's in it for us—these stories about someone else, these hundreds of pages of adversity and self-discovery, triumph and tarnish and gleam? These are other people's lives, after all. Strangers, mostly. People we'll never meet, people whose clocks most often keep on ticking, long after the last words have been inked. Sure, the form has had its fair share of bad press, thanks in no small part to the not-true "true" stories offered by the likes of James Frey's discredited addiction memoir *A Million Little Pieces*, and Herman Rosenblat's invented Holocaust love story *Angel at the Fence*. Sure, it's been furiously protested, as countless otherwise unknown writers have turned to memoir to package and parade their tall adventure, their unhappy childhood, their ghastly marriage, their misguided mother, their bad luck. Still, every single week a new batch of personal stories is released. Memoir isn't going anywhere.

So what does memoir offer? What can it yield? Why am I, after all these years, still reading it, teaching it, shaping it, seeking it? The answers are many, but here I offer just one: Because memoir at its very best is the start of a conversation. It makes its interest in readers explicit, offering not just a series of life events, but a deliberate suggestion of what it is to be a human being—to experience confusion, despair, hope, joy, and all that happens in between. True memoir is a singular life transformed into a signifying life. True memoir is a writer acknowledging that he or she is not the only one in the room.

Consider, for example, Jean-Dominique Bauby's international bestseller *The Diving Bell and the Butterfly*, which later became a major motion picture. It's a slender book—a mere 132 pages. It's a terrifying book, written by a man who, in December 1995, suffers a massive stroke that leaves him permanently paralyzed. Bauby is "locked in," unable to move or speak. It's his left eye that saves him—his left eye, which he relies on to blink at the slate of letters an assistant shares. Blink by blink, letter by letter, Bauby communicates his story. He was a famous magazine editor, we learn. He is trapped, we learn. But he is still alive—and still, miraculously, hopeful. And even though each word comes slowly, even though he has no words to spare, Bauby makes the explicit effort to tell us about ourselves. He looks up from where he is and acknowledges our presence.

Here Bauby is, in the early pages, communicating the possibility for epistemic peace in the face of an unspeakable tragedy:

You can visit the woman you love, slide down beside her and stroke her still-sleeping face. You can build castles in Spain, steal the Golden Fleece, discover Atlantis, realize your childhood dreams and adult ambitions.

Here he is, pages later, telling us what survival is, ensuring that we understand that sometimes anger is life-giving, too:

I need to feel strongly, to love and to admire, just as desperately as I need to breathe. A letter from a friend, a Balthus painting on a postcard, a page of Saint-Simon, give meaning to the passing hours. But to keep my mind sharp, to avoid descending into resigned indifference, I maintain a level of resentment and anger, neither too much nor too little, just as a pressure cooker has a safety valve to keep it from exploding.

If anyone has earned the right to self-absorption, it is Bauby. He cannot, after all, move or breathe or speak without the help of another, and he does not have long to live. But self-absorption is not his métier. All-consuming anger is not his mood. He does not expect, by the end of his book, to be congratulated for the losses he's endured. Bauby's interests extend far beyond the terrible thing that has radically rearranged his life. His ambitions are empathic ones. He writes so that we, his readers, might come to know that imagination is salvation, that we must trust the dreamworks in our heads.

Bauby, in short, wants to leave behind an artful record of what it is to live. He wants us to know hope, to imbibe it, even though his own existence is fragile. If you want more proof of Bauby's writerly generosity, look at his final passage. He's staring straight at us:

Does the cosmos contain keys for opening up my diving bell? A subway line with no terminus? A currency strong enough to buy my freedom back? We must keep looking. I'll be off now.

On an urban campus in Philadelphia, I sit with young people on the verge of adulthood, talking about the lives they've lived and the things that have mattered and the personal details from which stories are sprung. The talk, in my classroom, is about transcendence. It's about making the work bigger than the writer. The record is only the record, I say. Make the details speak for all of us.

It is all too tempting to allow that let-me-tell-my-story instinct to rule, all too easy to spend the time sussing out details, confirming chronologies, giving the whole thing some shine and some sass.

Memoirists must succumb to weeks, months, years spent examining (and cross-examining) themselves. But things grow claustrophobic—monochromatic, monologue-esque – when memoirists fail to say to the reader —one way or another—I know that you have lived your joys and sorrows, too. These are my lessons, for you.

Consider, now, Alice Sebold's *Lucky*, a book that begins with these lines:

This is what I remember: My lips were cut. I bit down on them when he grabbed me from behind and covered my mouth. He said these words: "I'll kill you if you scream." I remained motionless. "Do you understand? If you scream you're dead." I nodded my head. My arms were pinned to my sides by his right arm wrapped around me and my mouth was covered with his left.

Sebold will, over the course of her book, render every detail of this brutal, horrifying, unforgivable rape. She will tell us about the police and the hearing and the search for safety. She will share with us her slow return to the world:

I was dancing and falling in love. This time, a boy in Lila's math class: Steve Sherman. I told him about the rape after we had gone to see a movie and had a few drinks. I remember that he was wonderful with it, that he was shocked and horrified but comforting. He knew what to say. Told me I was beautiful, walked me home and kissed me on the cheek. I think he also liked taking care of me. By that Christmas, he became a fixture at our house.

This is Sebold's story. It's a riveting story. Reporting back must have been excruciating, and we deeply empathize; I profoundly do. But to read *Lucky* is to tunnel in so completely to another's tragedy that we forget—and are not encouraged to remember—the communality of survivors.

Personal, headline-making, loved by many, *Lucky* does not, nonetheless, transcend itself. We readers close the book knowing what happened to Sebold. We hold in our hands the blow-by-blow account, a strictly chronological retelling. This is a story about one, told by one. Its lessons—about victimhood, shame, justice, and living forward—may be suggested by the nature of the events, but they are never made explicit. Readers will not find deliberate signifiers here, nor expressly articulated universal truths. It's not a conversation, in other words, but a tragic (if quite important) story, well-told.

Kate Christensen's *Blue Plate Special: An Autobiography of My Appetites* is, for the most part, precisely what its title suggests—a reporting on Christensen's life story, amplified, along the way, by recipes, or, as the jacket copy puts it, "a narrative in which food—eating it, cooking it, reflecting on it—becomes the vehicle for unpacking a life." Christensen has an uneasy childhood. She has a raucous, unstable adolescence, a difficult time settling in as a young adult, a wild foray journey into middle age. She marries and loses that marriage. She falls in love with a man almost half her age. She finally publishes the novels she writes, to increasing acclaim.

Throughout it all, food is Christensen's salvation; it is her mecca, and the narrative's primary driver. But Christensen knows she's not the only woman who has ever leaned on food for emotional succor. Look, for example, at these words from the book's prologue. Food, Christensen is saying, embodies life lessons for us all.

To taste fully is to love fully. And to live fully is to be awake and responsible to complexities and truths—good and terrible, overwhelming and miniscule. To eat passionately is to allow the world in; there can be no hiding or sublimation when you're chewing a mouthful of food so good it makes you swoon.

Yeah, we say, when we read this. I'm in. For Christensen has opened a door; she has acknowledged us, has said, in so many words, I may be about to tell you a story that is all about me, but don't think that I've lost sight of the fact that food persuades and maps and consoles you, too. Christensen lifts her story toward something bigger, something signifying. She looks up and glances across her page. I see you, she says.

And we feel seen.

BORDER CROSSERS: THE HERE/THERE MEMOIRS

FIRST APPEARED IN *PUBLISHING PERSPECTIVES*

LET US RETURN to one of my favorite memoirs of all time—Michael Ondaatje's *Running in the Family*. I'll use any excuse, but this, I think, is a particularly good one.

We're in the first chapter, "Asia." We're reading the opening lines.

What began it all was the bright bone of a dream I could hardly hold onto. I was sleeping at a friend's house. I saw my father, chaotic, sur-rounded by dogs, and all of them were screaming and barking into the tropical landscape. The noises woke me. I sat on the uncomfortable sofa, and I was in a jungle, hot, sweating.

This is the late 1970s. Ondaatje is saturated with yearning. Born in Sri Lanka, relocated to Canada, it is time, he realizes, to go home again, to "travel back to the family I had grown from—those relations from my par-ents' generation who stood in my memory like frozen opera." Ondaatje's journey will become our journey—through time, with the assistance of maps, among the elevations and valleys of poems. A distant world will be rendered near. We will be enchanted, educated, *globalized* by the layer-ing in of the foreign and familiar.

All memoirists travel across the accordion folds of synapses and time. Border-crossing memoirists additionally move back and forth across space—past signposts, over deckled landmasses, into new weather, to-ward the science of geomorphology. Their points of view are duality inflected. Their vocabularies are exotic and hued. Their ideas about home are perforated and embellished by contrasts, contradictions, and corporeal compromise.

Do we come to know a place better once we leave it? What is the through line between beauty and ruin? What power do words have to resurrect that which is gone, and what of this mash of language that arises from those who have learned love in many places? Border-crossing memoirists—the best ones—wonder. They lessen geographic distance (for themselves, for their readers) by tendering juxtapositions. The remembered versus the known. The rumored versus the proven. The here versus the there.

In her National Book Critics Circle Award winning *Brother, I'm Dying,* Edwidge Danticat tells the story of a life lived in two countries, with two fathers—her biological father who moves from Haiti to New York City in pursuit of a better life for his family, and her second father, Uncle Joseph, who remains behind. Danticat herself will join her first family in New York City at the age of twelve. The primary action of this memoir will take place years later, when both fathers/brothers are dying and Danticat, pregnant with her first child, must reconcile the brothers' legacies.

Brother, I'm Dying slides back and forth between the life stories of brothers and the extraordinarily distinct geographies of Haiti and Brooklyn. It is a deeply researched book, "an attempt at cohesiveness, and at re-creating a few wondrous and terrible months when their lives and mine intersected in startling ways, forcing me to look forward and back at the same time." It is two brothers, two landscapes, one daughter in between. Danticat paints for us not just the vital, harsh, pocked chorography of each place, but the impact chorography has on character and fate. The contrasts educate us. The similarities break our hearts.

Much the same is at work in Anthony Shadid's *House of Stone.* This is the story of Shadid's return to the family home in Lebanon—the domicile of his great-grandfather Isber—and of his willing it to rise again from the dust. Shadid was, at the time, a *Washington Post* reporter with an

American wife and daughter. He became a man obsessed with somehow making "the statement to my daughter and her generation that Isber's house, whatever its condition, remained a home worth care." He plants a skinny olive tree and then, in a year, returns.

This ancestral house is riddled with ghosts. This memoirist is a man with "Oklahoma-accented Arabic, sprinkled with Egyptian colloquialisms"—at least half a foreigner, in other words. He brings the full force of his multiple dualities to the fabled portrait he paints. The passage I quote below, for example, is constructed of American similes and Arabic terms. It is at once evocative and instructive. It could have only been written by a writer who has touched down in many worlds—a committed border crosser.

Once utilitarian and still inescapably elegant, its stones ascended row after symmetrical row, thirty-five in all, ending with the armid, an Arabic word borrowed from Turkish that refers to those red tile shingles of a Levantine and cosmopolitan past. The roof was shored up by wood arches shaped like a study violin's scroll. The two balconies were girded by finely wrought but rusted iron railings perched over a burly plum tree. The larger of the balconies framed the most graceful feature of the house, the triple arches, buttressed by two marble columns. There is perhaps no feature that more forcefully evokes the notion of a traditional Lebanese house than the triple arcade, though inspiration for the design dates back nearly three millennia, to Roman antiquity.

Finally, let's consider what happens in *The Girl Who Fell to Earth*, by Sophia Al-Maria. Born to an American mother and a Bedouin father, sent off to Qatar to live as a teen with her father's family, Al-Maria takes us deep inside the private realms of desert dwellers, arranged marriages, *abaya* fittings, and Ladies' saloons. The book feels, at times, like an undercover mission, as this young woman with a keen eye, an American perspective, and a surfeit of questions about belonging reports back on a veiled world—vividly.

The "saloon" was like a grown-up clubhouse and bore a large warning, "No Men Allowed." The windows were papered over with posters of relaxing European women. It always looked kind of threatening to me. Like a meth lab with a no-trespassing sign put up my some paranoid hillbillies.... The main room was designed like a sala, with cushions lining the walls and magazines like Sayidaty and Snob al Hasna stacked in the corners. A hefty Jordanian woman sat immobile in the middle of the room, her ankles propped up on tissue boxes while she waited for elaborate trails of henna to dry.

Within a single paragraph we have encountered the mash of those Americanisms (meth lab, paranoid hillbillies) and those indigenous particulars (magazines like *Snob al Hasna* and the elaborate trails of henna). We have gone in deep, outfitted with helpful navigational tools—the looks like/sounds like stuff of a writer whose first language and first landscape will always afflict and affect her ways of seeing.

Committed border crossers. I look for them, when I read memoir, just as I turn toward the inherent possibilities of a more global perspective when I sit down to write. It's just one more way that we can help ensure that memoir, as a genre, remains relevant—more generous than simple autobiography, more meaningful than one-dimensional naval gazing, more artful than pure woe-is-me. It's one more way (though not the only way) that memoirists can broaden their engagement with the world—and leave their readers broadened, too.

ARTFUL DODGERS: ON THE POWER OF WHITE-SPACE MEMOIRS

FIRST APPEARED IN *CREATIVE NONFICTION*

WHAT YOU PUT IN. What you leave out. It all comes down to this—the leaving out part being the hardest part, the heart of the art that is memoir. Autobiography is what happened then, what happened next, what happened; it is bricks and butyl caulk. Not memoir. Memoir is distillation and sculpt, the places in between, a life cranked daringly apart: *What was it all about?* It is the chronology of ideas, and the supervalent thought, and the mind in pursuit of eloquent collisions. It is the air let into the tent.

Every memoir I read is a lesson in craft. Every memoir I own has been shuffled into taxa (childhood memoirs, illness memoirs, nature memoirs) and then shuffled once again (first-person memoirs, second-person memoirs, graphic-art memoirs), aligned and subsequently exiled. Lately I've grown increasingly intrigued by what I think of as the artful dodgers, those memoirs that do more with the void than most memoirs dare do. Those memoirs written by memoirists who have, in some exceptionally brilliant way, trusted the reader with secret unsaids.

Take Paula Fox in *Borrowed Finery*, a memoir written late in life to capture a well-loved writer's "highly unusual beginnings." Fox was the daughter of a mother and a father who were immune to the idea of parental sacrifice. She was born and then soon shuttled off to live with whomever might have her—Uncle Elwood, the gentle pastor; Candelaria, the Cuban grandmother; Mrs. Lesser, a friend of the mother; and etcetera. Every now and then the mother and father would appear—the father more than the mother, both characters an exercise in bewilderment (at best) and in psychological abuse (by most people's standards). Yanked across the country, into Cuba, up to Montreal, from one school to another, Fox was denied both continuity and reliable companionship. If anyone had earned the right to moan in memoir, it was Fox. But that's the thing: she doesn't.

Indeed, *Borrowed Finery* is a tour-de-force of self-restraint—a hammering in of landscape and incident until the fractured childhood miraculously coheres. Fox tells us what she remembers, and what she doesn't, leaving white spaces in between to mark the broken time. But the true white space here is Fox's refusal to condemn the parents who condemned her to such a fate. That's because Fox (unbeknownst to us) is reckoning with something bigger here, something she will not reveal until her memoir's very end. Fox, like her mother, gave birth to a baby quite young. Fox, like her mother, left a daughter to questions. "It was a hopeless wish that I would discover why my birth and my existence were so calamitous for my mother," Fox writes early—a line that means infinitely more when we encounter the memoir's final pages. *Borrowed Finery*, a memoir saturated with the details of place, person, and thing, is stunningly silent on matters of accusation and retribution. Fox's white space leaves us room to intuit. It ensures that we do not cast easy blame.

Calvin Trillin's childhood was as different from Fox's as any childhood could be. He was the son of Jewish grocer, a boy who knew where home was and what the future likely held. "The man was stubborn," Trillin's *Messages from My Father* begins. "Take the coffee incident." Eight simple words, and we know that we're in for a life story that is infinitely playful, probably honoring. This father has his quirks, but he makes his children laugh. This father isn't a Big Somebody, but he keeps his son in food, clothes, and dreams of matriculation at Yale.

The easy sway of Trillin's language lulls us. We take the father as he comes—stubborn, taciturn, a man who "did not make a strong first impression," a collector of yellow-hued ties, a person with a secret knack for rhyming ditties, the sort who would ask anyone fluent in a foreign language to translate "The left-handed lizard climbed up the eucalyptus tree and ate a persimmon." Where is it all going? It's sweet. We read along. And then suddenly it hits us—this Not a Big Somebody is Damned Important after all. He has an ethos that we—blindsided, entering through Trillin's carefully hinged and hung back door—have absorbed. "You might as well be a mensch," the Jewish grocer is reported saying, and suddenly we the readers want to be a mensch most of all. Suddenly all this funny business is meaning business. We are left admiring goodness most of all—a lesson held in the book's generous margins.

I found Chris Offutt's *The Same River Twice* in a used bookstore; it strikes me as infinitely timeless. It is a woven tale, a past tense/present tense rotation between Offutt's hobo years on the road and his time in the woods just ahead of the birth of his first son. Violent, vulgar, weird, beautiful, squirming, festering, wild—the whole works like some encrusted poem. We know a baby will be born by the time this memoir finds its end, but Offutt nevertheless holds us in supreme suspense, for the young man that Offutt tells us he was doesn't seem destined to survive his own severe wanderlust, his inability to stay put or out of trouble. "I hope for a son who is not like me," Offutt writes, in the woods, in the present tense. "... the journal was my life, and the rest of existence only fiction," Offutt remembers himself thinking, back then.

It's between the alternating past and present that Offutt lodges his white space. It's how he doesn't feel the need to *explain* how that feral man became this husband and near father. Offutt just tells us the stories and lets them collide, refuting the possibility of an unshakable conclusion and leaving the messy things messy. "I think of all the things I want to tell him, and say nothing," Offutt writes in the epilogue. Exactly. The power of white space.

I'm almost out of room, and so, then, briefly, finally: Patti Smith and *Woolgathering*. A tiny book that traces and briefly tethers that which is considered, that which is remembered, that which is wished for. Patti Smith, the great punk rocker poetess photographer friend, produced, with *Woolgathering*, a brief memoir of awe. She leads the way but does not direct, leaving us with lines like these: "And I wandered among them (the woolgatherers), through thistle and thorn, with no task more exceptional than to rescue a fleeting thought, as a tuft of wool, from the comb of the wind."

How ambiguous is that, and how surreally lovely? It is white, white, white; it is spectacularly wide open.

FINDING EMPATHY IN THE ESSAY

_____

FIRST APPEARED IN *CHICAGO TRIBUNE*

IN 1988, ROBERT ATWAN, series editor of *The Best American Essays*, made this provocative pronouncement: "Never before—except perhaps in the days of Emerson and Thoreau—have so many fine writers begun to explore (the essay's) literary possibilities."

Annie Dillard. William H. Gass. Stephen Jay Gould. Gore Vidal. Gerald Early. Cynthia Ozick. Joseph Brodsky. The world had been summoned by seers and prophets.One quarter of a century later, the ravishing seductions of the essayistic "I" continue to snare the wily, ingenious, sensual and playful. Charles D'Ambrosio. Claudia Rankine. Eula Biss. Ander Monson. Lia Purpura. Rebecca Solnit. Leslie Jamison. Megan Stielstra. Meghan Daum. Stephanie LaCava. Elif Batuman. I truncate the list; the point is: the essay swivels on.

But what does it matter what any of them think about the spires of Warsaw or Panera Bread, the Aragon or mentorship, the color blue, a strand of pearls, a summer in Samarkand? Why should we care about their digressive curiosities? Because there, right there, in their meander and jig, lie the implosive possibilities of our worlds and ourselves. It's in the accordion folds of the empathetic imagination.

If, as Terrence Des Pres once wrote: "Imagination does its work by seeing what's there," looking well is the first imperative of the empathetic essayist. Looking toward a transporting beyond. Here is Lia Purpura in a too-bright room, in an essay entitled "Autopsy Report":

I shall begin with the chests of drowned men, bound with ropes and die-sel-slicked. Their ears sludge-filled. Their legs mud-smeared. Asleep below deck when a freighter hit and the river rose inside their tug. Their lashes white with river silt.

The diesel, the sludge, the mud: this is the actuality of what Purpura sees—the reportable evidence. The men asleep, the river rising: This is her transcending beyond the facts, the view that only her imagination can yield. In opening her eyes, Purpura has opened her heart. She has tilted the scene toward the beginning of its end.

In introducing the "scrappy incondite essays" of his new collection, "Loi-tering," Charles D'Ambrosio tells us that "behind each piece, animating every attempt, is the echo of a precarious faith, that we are more inti-mately bound to one another by our kindred doubts than our brave con-clusions." In richly brocaded prose, D'Ambrosio deals in the tremulous and uncertain. His language slides and slides down alternative trajectories.

In the essay "This Is Living," for example, D'Ambrosio reconstructs a father few sons could readily understand or forgive—a father whose own violent childhood did not preclude him from wielding a shocking vio-lence of his own. D'Ambrosio's father once witnessed the beating of an uncle and ran. D'Ambrosio, the author, is now in perpetual pursuit:

Now whenever I visit Chicago I make the same run myself, chasing after my father, pursuing him all the way down Argyle, crossing the Outer Drive until I too hit the lake. My father doesn't know I do this, and he probably wouldn't care or even understand, and really, I have no idea why this lunatic errand matters to me, beyond the foolish belief that, one of these days, when I reach the lake's edge, I will find him, I mean literally find him, still there, an eleven year old boy, cold and alone, with nowhere else to run.

D'Ambrosio's empathetic imagination is an appeasing imagination. It is the arrow hurtling back toward what might have been/will never be.

While D'Ambrosio chases a past that will never fully be summoned, Megan Stielstra, in an essay called "Wake the Goddamn World," chases a better self. She is in Prague when we meet her. She has wakened to a fight in a street. There are plenty of reasons to do nothing, and nothing is what Stielstra does. But as Stielstra leaves that apartment for the final time, when she finds the victim in the lobby, Stielstra "in (her) memory" apologizes—"digging through our shared patchwork language to find the right words: *I'm so sorry. I should have done better. I will do better.* I tell her how, this time, I will rush down the four flights of stairs and put my body between them. This time, I will rush down the four flights of stairs—not in time to stop it, but still in time to help, to get her to a hospital, or a friend's, or a shelter. This time ... I'll wake the goddamn world."

Stielstra's essay—and her imagination—leave her fictively ennobled. The distance between the facts and her yearning to change those facts is where her redemption lies.

For Eula Biss in "The Balloonists," a book about family and fractures and the mother who left, the empathetic imagination emerges from an exploration of insufficient evidence. Biss performs the rational/irrational calculus of "if this, then possibly that." Her process is one of extrapolation – the delicate sidestep from the quasi-remembered toward the conjecture:

I think I remember the sound of my mother typing in the basement. But this is only because I know there was a typewriter down there. I don't know how much she used it. She was almost always home, but if she wasn't typing and she wasn't in the garden and she wasn't putting bread in the oven, what was she doing?

What was she doing? Where the empathetic imagination ends, compassion begins.

In "Citizen: An American Lyric," a jagged evocation of life in our seething, unjust world, Claudia Rankine works by way of implication, replacing, in the first long sweep of her pages, the *I* with a *You* until the reader is not quite sure of who the reader is—the injured or the injuring. Unsettled, uprooted, we, the readers, become the agents of empathy, entrusted with the responsibility of seeing, feeling, knowing:

You are twelve attending Sts. Philip and James School on White Plains Road and the girl sitting in the seat behind asks you to lean to the right during exams so she can copy what you have written. Sister Evelyn is in the habit of taping the 100s and the failing grades to the coat closet doors. The girl is Catholic with waist-length brown hair. You can't remember her name: Mary? Catherine?

You never really speak except for the time she makes her request and later when she tells you you smell good and have features more like a white person. You assume she thinks she is thanking you for letting her cheat and feels better cheating from an almost white person.

In "The Empathy Exams," the title essay in Leslie Jamison's collection, Jamison is a "medical actor," a young woman who performs acts of unwellness in order to further the education of aspiring doctors. Jamison is also a young woman who has recently undergone both an abortion and heart surgery. Jamison isn't just circling the literal and literary possibilities of empathy here. She is overtly addressing the condition, suggesting that it operates as a cascade. Her empathic imagination is a historian, a chronicler. It is a spiral without an end.

Empathy requires inquiry as much as imagination. Empathy requires knowing you know nothing. Empathy means acknowledging a horizon of context that extends perpetually beyond what you can see: an old woman's gonorrhea is connected to her guilt is connected to her marriage is connected to her children is connected to the days when she was a child. All this is connected to her domestically stifled mother, in turn, and to her parents' unbroken marriage; maybe everything traces its roots to her very first period, how it shamed and thrilled her.

Finally, in "Cousins," Jo Ann Beard suggests that the empathetic imagination does its best work under the cover of stopped time. This is an essay, despite its title, that is mostly about two sisters, one of whom is the author's mother. In discontinuous, highly evocative scenes, Beard gives us the family history. Early on, during a happily remembered parade, she tosses the "silver hyphen" of a baton to the sky and lets it linger "for a moment against the sun." Ultimately the baton falls, time moves forward, and we find ourselves in a hospital room—the aunt smoking, the mother dying, the morphine doing its work:

My mother sleeps silently while my aunt thinks. As the invisible hands tend to her, she dives and comes up, breaks free of the water. A few feet over a fish leaps again, high in the air. Her arms move lazily back and forth, holding her up, and as she watches, the fish is transformed. High above the water, it rises like a silver baton, presses itself against the blue August sky, and refuses to drop back down.

Refuses to drop back down. There it is—the wide open forever, the eternal beyond. Beard's stopped time makes room for all of us. We bow our heads. We link our arms. We stand seeing what Beard herself could not have seen, but what might have been, what perhaps must have been, the image and the prayer, the hope, that we will only ever find in our collective and empathetic imagining.

A WRITER LEARNS FROM WYETH

FIRST APPEARED IN *WOVEN TALE PRESS*

ANDREW WYETH would have turned one hundred this year, but I like to think about him young. Planting his toy soldiers in the battle-scarred hills of his childhood home in Chadds Ford, Pennsylvania. Covertly sketching in the shadows of the Kuerner farm. Scrambling up from the creek as a cartoon Robin Hood, his band of followers in mud-sloshing pursuit.

Physically fragile, imaginatively robust, Wyeth had a wild appetite for the summoned up; he placed an antic trust in fantasy. As the youngest of five in the N.C. Wyeth clan, he was famously left mostly to his own intense devices—occasionally tutored, never formally schooled. It was Peter Hurd, according to Richard Meryman's *Andrew Wyeth: A Secret Life*, who discovered the cost of such liberation. On the verge of becoming Wyeth's brother-in-law, Hurd was, Meryman writes, "the first person in the family to notice or care that Andy was not entirely literate. When Peter asked him to look up something in the encyclopedia under F, Andrew was helpless."

Andrew was twelve years old at the time. He would eventually learn the hooks and squiggles, crosses and dots of the American alphabet. But he would always prefer, Meryman tells us, the sound of a story being read out loud to the labor of personally deciphering the letters on the page. He would also never forget the felt shame of knowing less.

And yet—perhaps ironically—there is much to be learned about the literary arts from Andrew Wyeth. There are, to begin with, the stories delivered to us through his pencil, charcoal, watercolor, drybrush, and tempera. The stories on paper and canvas and boards.

Recently, on a storm-slung day, I lived (it seemed I lived) many of those narratives while standing in the darkened rooms at the Brandywine River Museum of Art, which, together with the Seattle Art Museum, has produced *Andrew Wyeth: In Retrospect* (through September 17, 2017). There's the window through which the breeze is blowing—lifting up, absconding with the seasons of a long, stark friendship ("Wind from the Sea"). This painting is a pause, I imagined; it is an interlude, it is a secret start of something.

There are the deadly hooks above the steely head of a former German soldier—and not just the hooks, but the fault lines, the cracks in the past of the man ("Karl, 1948"). Each crack a chapter, I imagined. Or a verse. What would it be to write the verse?

There are the flurries of snow that refuse to die white on the brown-bruised earth ("Snow Flurries"), and when I asked myself why the snow refused to die, I had, it seemed to me, a story. But it's when we read what Wyeth said—to his wife, to Thomas Hoving (in *Andrew Wyeth: Autobiography*), to Meryman, to Edward Hopper, to anyone who could persuade Wyeth to step, for a moment, out of the shadows he preferred and into the concentrated light of reminisce and explanation—that we discover the painter who might have offered a master class on the asterisk arts of literature. The necessary unseens. The rites of passage. The principled purpose.

Advice on where the story might be found, from Wyeth: "I've often thought that I've built my career on happening to find things that are suddenly unusual. Of course, it's what you seek and what you grasp as an opportunity and follow up on again and again that really does it."

Advice on when to set the story in motion: "I may be walking from the bathroom down to the kitchen. Or I may be walking over the hill. I may be driving the car too fast. And I'll get this idea, this emotion that I've been thinking about for a long time, perhaps something has sparked it off, it's a feeling that I've always felt about something, and I'll say 'Jesus, this is terrific.' And I may hold it back, purposefully for a while, before I even put it on a piece of paper or on a panel. I think timing is very important in this thing."

Advice on complexity: "I feel that the simpler the thing, the more complex it is bound to be."

Advice on the story, pursued: "The only thing I want to search for is the growth and depth of my emotion toward a given object. In that way I free myself from the bonds of routine technical quality."

Advice on the narrative ideal: "I would like to try to paint so nothing is at rest in my work. Nothing is frozen. I would like people to sense even in those paintings with brilliant passages of sunlight, that the sunlight is not really still but that you can really see the passage of the sun."

Advice on revision: "I obtain great excitement in the changes. Because with them, the painting begins to discover itself. It begins to roll. It's like a snowball rolling down the hill."

Advice on fighting the demoralizing flavors du jour, the hyping critics, the numbing public: "I do not feel we should make our cause by letters or protest but should strengthen it by better painting."

Wyeth was a man of secrets and distortions. He cherished the dirty page, the already smudged or time-scuffed canvas. He had learned painterly technique, at last, standing at his famous father's side—the fall of light, the roundness of a shoulder, the pliable anatomy of a spine—only to discover that it's the emotion of the thing that matters most, the private ideals and fantasies you invest in every stroke, the story you are desperate to tell yourself...and not the given rules of the trade.

Reality plied with mystery: that's what Wyeth discovered and that's what he teaches. Mystery pushed past careful equanimity, toward the danger of finding out, of actually, inexcusably knowing: Why does the curtain lift? Where do the cracks begin, and do they end? Why won't the snow finally die?

A year ago, I piled every book I owned onto the family room floor and made a choice about which would stay and which would go. Eliminated: the memoirs that dishonor the form, the bypassed histories, the novels I never did choose for myself, the volumes that seemed to grow more pale, obtuse, self-congratulatory, market-primed, or turgid with every page I turned. Returned to their shelves: The books whose streets I've walked, whose people I've fiercely loved, whose poems have tamed my migraines, whose pages I read to my son and still, in the early morning, wish to read to myself.

Looking now at what remains I am struck by a deep abiding sense that Andrew Wyeth would approve. That he would wish to be read to by these authors—Michael Ondaatje, Alice McDermott, Kent Haruf, Louise Erdrich, Fae Myenne Ng, Paul Horgan, Willa Cather, Helen Macdonald, James Baldwin, Sallie Tisdale, Chloe Aridjis, Jayne Anne Phillips, Jane Mendelsohn, Toni Morrison, Anthony Doerr, Jack Gilbert, Terry Tempest Williams, Olivia Laing, Paul Lisicky, Patti Smith, W.G. Sebald, Seamus Deane, Nell Leyshon, Elizabeth Strout, Alyson Hagy, Wallace Stegner, Eudora Welty, Ian McEwan, Ta-Nehisi Coates, Marilynne Robinson, Colum McCann, Alison Bechdel, Stefan Hertmans, Terrence Des Pres, Stacey D'Erasmo, Virginia Woolf, William Faulkner, Kim Echlin, F. Scott Fitzgerald, Mark Haddon, Raymond Carver, Abigail Thomas, Annie Dillard, Chloe Honum, Colm Tóibín, Megan Stielstra, Gerald Stern, Ernest Hemingway—who found the quick startle of an idea and then held back until the story or the poem commanded its first sentence. These authors who have built their tales from the simple, complex web of the barely sayable, the crushingly true, the innately grasped for, the lift in the curtain.

These authors who hold their own amidst the tyranny of common desire and uncommon generosity. These authors who choose the time-scuffed page to put down things as they are because soon (look, the moment is gone), they will never be again.

Find a ruined canvas, and ruin it more, Wyeth teaches. Tip the story out of balance so that it will be more true. Write from the urgent place of your most terrible love, your most delicate secret, your anger and your gratitude for having been neglected so that you might be set free. Teach your heart to see what your eyes cannot. Make the people in your stories vulnerable to the places they come from, the places they leave, the places they return to. Come back to it, come back to it, come back to it, then leave it. Done. You will be exhausted. You will be a writer. You will find the picture in your thousand words.

HERE IS THE NEEDLE, THIS IS THE THREAD: 'SAFEKEEPING' AND THE LIBERATION OF MEMOIR

FIRST APPEARED IN *THE MILLIONS*

MEMOIR HAS EMERGED as a liberated species—breaking its own rules so repeatedly that there are now no rules except (for purists) to tell the truth and (for everyone else) to foil narcissism. The memoirist's page is malleable. The memoirist's frame endlessly shatters.

There are plenty of examples, but I like these: Joan Wickersham built *The Suicide Index* out of shifting perspectives, drawing on fiction, even, when she could not explain her father's self-destruction. Maggie Nelson offered 240 numbered, jostled, jostling, perhaps not seamless blue-tinted paragraphs in *Bluets*. Darin Strauss delivered *Half a Life* with many half white pages. Mark Richard wrote his *House of Prayer No. 2* in second person, save for an opening gambit in mostly third. Terry Tempest Williams, in *When Women Were Birds: Fifty-Four Variations on Voice*, yielded, to the reader, many consecutive pages of white, white, white—in imitation of her own mother's blank journals—before she went on to meditate about voice, but not in any programmatic order.

Sarah Manguso stitched *Ongoingness: The End of a Diary* out of the piecemeal fabric of obsession. Heidi Julavits constructed *The Folded Clock* as a diary whose pages have been shuffled—a diary out of sequence. Jeannie Vanasco forged *The Glass Eye* out of "several color-coded binders labeled 'Dad,' 'Mom,' 'Jeanne,' and 'Mental Illness.'"

And in *Heating & Cooling: 52 Micro-Memoirs,* Beth Ann Fennelly compiled a scrapbook of small thoughts and big—a slender book of sometimes one-page flicks on topics like married love and children.

Life is iterative. Memoir is. No two stories can be the same true stories. And while it might seem today that all of this is obvious, that memoir *must* be plastic, it actually wasn't nearly as obvious 18 years ago when Abigail Thomas—a writer known for her fiction, a woman known for her wit—published a collection of true stories called *Safekeeping.* It wasn't a usual true-story book. It was declined, Thomas has said, by many a publishing house.

There was, to begin with, no "after that happened, then this." There was no pronouncement of a thesis. There wasn't even a profusion of I's (there were far more she's), and though the whole thing seemed casual enough—no footnotes, no pretense, no unforsaken woe—the casual had been run through an intensifying rinse. These pages read like poems, but there were no line breaks. These lines kicked as if they'd been enjambed, but where were the enjambments?

Instead there was the hard knock of nouns. The slide of simple accountings. Sleight-of-hand suspense. A division into thirds, by which I mean sections titled "Before," "Mortality," and "Here and Now." Meditations on, well, married love and children. Thomas could make you think that she was just delivering the facts of her life—three kids before the age of 26, three marriages, grief, passing conversations with a sister—as they occurred to her, but no. She was *arranging* them.

The book's first paragraph suspends time and keeps it suspended so that time becomes everything that might have been and the things that actually were, what never came to pass and what hasn't happened yet. It's a magic trick. There's a white bird, winging:

Before I met you I played my music on a child's Victrola. I played Music from Big Pink *over and over. "Tears of Rage." "The Weight."* Wheels of Fire. *I had three kids. We ate on the overturned kitchen drawer because I didn't have a table. I was young. I didn't know what things could happen. I spent my time in the moment; everything else was shoved ahead, like furniture I didn't need yet. We were crammed into a small space. My bed was in the living room.*

Safekeeping sidesteps the blunt force of a directed narrative. It's happenstance, with a purpose. The reader has to pay attention. On a page titled "Tomorrow," it has been, Thomas writes in first person, a year since her second husband died—the husband she loved best when they were no longer married but (somehow) friends. On the next page, titled "Witness to His Life," this second husband is remembered as alive, a first-person remembering about a restaurant. Next we have "When He Told Her," which recalls the time this second husband was, again, alive, but relating the news of his cancer. "When He Told Her" is a third-person remembrance. It would silence the author, we sense, if the chosen pronoun were an I. Its opening line: "She didn't really believe it, not really, not in her heart of hearts."

We don't understand our earlier selves, or we fear them, or we miss them, or we idolize the choices they didn't make. In *Safekeeping*, Thomas's earlier self is often a third-person self, because it's often a truer true story that way. And when the truth cannot even be guessed at, it is not guessed at. *Safekeeping*, then, is also a book of blank spaces, an emptiness between micro-fullness.

Marcel Proust and Karl Ove Knausgaard and other autobiographical inclusionists notwithstanding, memoir making is all about the needle and the thread, the patchwork and the patches, the careful stitchery. Memoir making is as much about *how* we remember as *what* we remember, and there's no better exemplar of that fact, now or then, to my way of thinking, than Thomas's *Safekeeping* and the two subsequent, equally brilliant Thomas memoirs: *A Three Dog Life* and *What Comes Next and*

How to Like It.

This isn't to suggest, of course, that previous memoirists have not played, for example, with point of view. bell hooks, for example, announces her methodology right up front in her memoir of childhood,

Bone Black:

Laying out the groundwork of my early life like a crazy quilt, Bone Black *brings together fragments to make a whole. Bits and pieces connect in a random and playfully irrational way. And there is always the persistence of repetition, for that is what the mind does—goes over and over the same things looking at them in different ways. The prevailing perspective is always that of the intuitive and critically thinking child mind. Sometimes memories are presented in third person, indirectly, just as all of us sometimes talk about things that way. We look back as if we are standing at a distance.*

But *Bone Black* is a childhood story, with a more or less chronological through line. *Safekeeping*, with its drifting time and shifting moods and searing gentleness, is un-diagrammable, self-forgiving. Reading *Safekeeping* is like reading Carole Maso's *AVA*, a morning, afternoon, and night novel that ticks out the last-day memories of a dying 39-year-old professor of comparative lit. *AVA* stacks impressions, one upon the other. The sequenced lines are tethered to nothing but lifting desire:

Each holiday celebrated with real extravagance. Birthdays. Independence days. Saints' days. Even when we were poor. With verve.

Come sit in the morning garden for awhile.

Olives hang like earrings in late August.

It's up to the reader of *AVA* to fill in the blanks. It's up to Thomas's readers, too. We are forced to be smarter than we are.

Safekeeping is scrapbook and seam. It is ephemera if words can be called ephemera. It is wisdom without the baggage of authority. "Like most power it was utterly real and utterly illusory," Thomas writes toward the end, about her younger, beautiful self. "But she spent the next forty years with her eye on who was looking back. This didn't get in her way. It was her way. Her ambition was to be desired. Now it's over and what a relief. Finally she can get some work done."

Abigail Thomas placed her unassuming trust in her own ideas about linearity and urgency, dodge and confession, frame and voice, and maybe she didn't know at first what she was making, but she made it anyway. Her words were her needle. Her life was her thread. Some of her stitches looped and some of them frayed and sometimes there was a break in the pattern. Life's like this, Thomas instructed. Life is everything. Life can be made and it can be unmade, too.

Go on, she said. You try it.

She unbuttoned a button. She unbuttoned another. We grew less and less encumbered.

RAW TO THE BONE: TRANSPORTED BY SPRINGSTEEN'S RIVER SONGS

FIRST APPEARED IN *POETS' QUARTERLY*

MIGHT AS WELL START WITH "SHENANDOAH," the old pioneer song that Springsteen and the Seeger Sessions Band transformed into sweet bitters in the living room of Springsteen's fabled New Jersey farmhouse. "Shenandoah," the tenth song on the *We Shall Overcome/Seeger Sessions* album, is music being made, as Springsteen himself has said. Music created in the moment, held between teeth, conducted with the frayed bracelet strings of an uplifted hand. It's music hummed, hymned, and high in the shoulder blades, deep in the blue pulse of a straining vein. Patti's lighting candles in the darkening farmhouse, as the band tunes in. The antique clock ticks. The thickly framed mirror doubles the volumes of sound and space. And now the Shenandoah roves.

Oh Shenandoah,

I long to see you,

Away you rolling river.

Oh Shenandoah,

I long to see you,

Away, I'm bound away,

'cross the wide Missouri

"Shenandoah" is a song without a known history. It is silt and residue, and it may not wash us clean, but it will wash us new. It is a river song, and if nobody knows who wrote it, that doesn't matter now. Springsteen and the Sessions Band have played it, they have made it, and so we live it true. We long to see that river, wide. We're bound, and bound away.

"Most of my songs are on the near banks of a river," Springsteen once said. In my own too-many-decades appreciation of Springsteen music, it is the explicit river that regenerates, restores, and blessedly unmoors me. It's Mary, the union card, and the wedding in "The River." It's "the groom standing alone beneath a weepin' willow tree," watching "the river rush so effortlessly" in "Reason to Believe." It's the "cry of the river" in "Valentine's Day," and the river growing wider in "Soul Driver" and the "whispering tide" of "Tomorrow Never Knows." It is as well the river that "narrows to a creek, that turns shallow and sandy" in "Long Time Coming."

It's also the river of "If I Should Fall Behind"—an unrighteous holy ask of forgiveness song, a some time in the evening song. The river, for Springsteen, signifies. Catholic and practically steepled, it is the place where people lie down to dream. It is where black feathers float and the moon rests and trouble runs wide beneath bird song. Springsteen's rivers are catalytic, confessional, a crawl and a hurry, weatherized and alive between the banks of assonance and disrepair. They will or they will not be crossed, but they will take us to the edge of things, to fractured landscapes and underground springs. Breaking, renewing, unmasking, abrading, Springsteen's rivers leave us raw to the bone.

Raw to the bone. I'm talking about vulnerability and exposure. I'm talking about reckoning, and so I am talking about that place where truth is found and memory thrives. Bruce Springsteen's personal truths and memories, of course. But also, I would like to make the claim, ours.

"Most of my music is emotionally autobiographical," Springsteen has said. "That's how they know I'm not kidding."

Exactly. He's not kidding, and we do know it, and in the company of Springsteen's own liturgical honesty—those lyrics he first scrawls across his journals with those high, looping h's, t's, and d's; those orchestrations that emerge with time and erode with time—we are, at least while the music plays, more honest, too. We allow ourselves to feel. We allow ourselves to move. We yield to time, to ache, to regret, to story, and also, because this is Springsteen, hope. In making room for Springsteen's mythic characters and worn-down crevasses—in allowing them in—we make room for our own authentic selves.

Let me explain:

I have stood and will stand, many a time, in my family room—different family rooms, different houses—with other people's stories on the embanking shelves, a 200-year-old spinning wheel against one wall, and Springsteen music on. It will be dark, and I will be alone. Beyond the windows, sometimes, if the moon is full, I'll see the lit eyes of a deer or, once, a fox. I'll see the twitch of a rabbit stopped, for that split instant, by the throbbing of a Springsteen river song.

The music will rise through the soles of my feet. It will scour, channel, silt, and further rise. In the dark cavern of my hips it will catch and swish. Outside, perhaps, the stars have come up, and probably the deer have vanished, and maybe the cicadas are rumbling around in their own mangled souls. But inside, a river churns, widens, roars, and steeps, and I am dancing Springsteen.

It is in this place that I have found memory and staked truth. Within this church, beneath this weather, beside the tapped roots and the floated feather. The first inklings of my poems have erupted here. The saturated hues of the characters that eventually amble their way to my novels. The ties that bind the remembered things that constitute my memoirs. I wrote my own river book—*Flow: The Life and Times of Philadelphia's Schuylkill River*—while keeping company with Springsteen songs. I gave my river her own voice so that she could gloat and lament and suffer and, finally, sing.

Much has been said about the community that Bruce Springsteen has both sought and forged. Much, too, has been said about the ranging democracy of his music—the folk, rock, country, jazz, blues; the symphonies and the solos. And while some of the great critics and commentators of our time— Jon Landau, Neil Strauss, Bobbie Ann Mason, Andrew Greeley, A.O. Scott, Nick Hornby, David Remmick—have pondered Springsteen, perhaps even nearly understood him, it is Springsteen himself whom we trust to explain Springsteen and to explicate the legacy he hopes to leave behind.

"I was interested in becoming part of people's lives, and hopefully, growing up with them—growing up together," he has written. And: "... music is primarily an emotional language; whatever you've written lyrically almost always comes in second to what the listener is feeling."

And: "I'm a romantic. To me the idea of a romantic is someone who sees the reality, lives the reality everyday, but knows about the possibilities, too. You can't lose sight of the dream." And, famously: "I wanted to invent a dance with no exact steps."

Springsteen has said all that and then, speaking to us in a language that bears no interpretation, he has sung: *Oh down to the river we ride.*

We don't need perfection from our rock-and-roll heroes. We don't want authority. We want, most of all, to believe. That he has thought about how he has lived. That he has noticed and empathized with those living around him. That he has driven this country and walked these landscapes and surrendered to the mighty minds, passions, yearnings of rivers. Springsteen makes the search for truth seem plausible, noble, even. And in doing so he inspires our own muddy, messy, necessary questing.

We learn, in the process, how right it feels to get out in front of our pretending and to be just who we are, our native, undecorated, unrighteous holy selves.

RECLAIMING A BELOVED WRITER FROM THE BRINK OF DISAPPEARANCE

———

FIRST APPEARED IN *LITHUB*

IN EARLY MARCH 1995 I wrote a letter to Paul Horgan and sent it off to Middletown, CT, where—following a polymathic career as a teacher, novelist, historian, biographer, short story writer, critic, appreciator, museum president, children's writer, two-time Pulitzer Prize winner, and recipient of more than four dozen additional honors—Horgan had been living.

I had been lost inside his *Richard Trilogy*, I explained. I was only just emerging. Maybe I would never fully emerge. Maybe I would never not ache as I then ached from the glorious, quiet trauma of reading his pages about a boy named Richard who accumulates, in mostly small but always terrifying ways, the revenants of shame. The drowning of a kitten. An awful eavesdropping. A paralysis before a cousin's madness, a dalliance with a murderer, a secret kept for a dying father.

Shame is a progressive tick. In Horgan's *Richard Trilogy*, shame is alive and advancing.

I want you to know, I wrote, I confessed.

Writing letters to writers whose work I loved was what I did back then—not a lot, but sometimes. It was the conversation I dared to imagine with a community—*Literature*—that lay mostly beyond my yearning reach. I had been raised responsibly to be responsible. I had studied the history and sociology of science as an undergrad, hiding my poems. I had started a business, I was raising a son, and the closest I was getting to literary community was a lovely bit of reckless scheming that converted a handful of family vacations into writing workshop sagas. My secret life was the words that others wrote, the dialogue I wished I was having.

I want you to know.

Horgan died within days of my mailing that letter. Cardiac arrest. He was 91 years old—"the writer's writer, the biographer's biographer," in the words of David McCullough; "that rarest of birds," said Walker Percy; the story finder and teller often compared to Henry James, Leo Tolstoy, and Thomas Hardy. In memoriam, I filled my library with more Paul Horgan. I searched for others with whom I might light the Horgan flame.

Have you read Paul Horgan? I would ask writers, when I did meet them. I would search for new analyses of his work, fresh appraisals, contemporary commentary on the body of work produced by a man who, in the words of Joseph Reed, writing Horgan's obituary for the *Independent*, seemed, to those who had known him, to be "immortal."

It wasn't until several years after Horgan's death that Loyola Classics Series editor Amy Welborn read *Things as They Are* for the first time, at the suggestion of George Weigel. But even that was just a lucky break for Horgan's legacy. "We were completely taken with it," Welborn wrote, "and astonished that it had slipped out of almost everyone's consciousness in the half-century since its publication."

If today there is a scattering of Goodreads and Amazon reviews on Horgan's work, if some of his work is still in print, if there are scholars of the American west still honoring Horgan's historic quests, Horgan's "disappearance from public, if not critical, appreciation," to quote Daniel J. Heisey in *Homiletic & Pastoral Review,* only seems to intensify as the years tick on. When I have studied him I have studied him alone.

I study his capacity to eulogize landscape: "Here and there a red gully lay, dry, ravaged by past cloudbursts." (*The Thin Mountain Air*)

His piercing physicalities: "His forehead was low, with a bony scowl that could not be changed. His nose was blunt, with its nostrils showing frontward." (*Things as They Are*)

His articulated angst: "But I fell in love with somebody different every day, and nobody ever knew it. It was an exhausting profusion of passions, and I concluded that nobody else in the world, behind all their smiling or preoccupied or sorrowing faces, knew as much as I did about what life was actually like . . ." (*Everything to Live For*)

His translation of a painted canvas into alphabetic words: "In them was an implied mourning for girlhood and its knowledge beyond innocence, overlaid with a lyric prophecy of the decay which however distant must overtake all things." (*Henriette Wyeth: The Artifice of Blue Light*)

Studying Horgan has served as a lifeline to my own work, to my own incessant quest to see and be and believe, to find and write the truth. At the same time, studying Horgan has impressed upon me the nagging actuality that the greatest among us can slip—so easily, so readily, so steadily, so surreally—from popular view.

It's a question, isn't it, or one of them, anyway—how some writers are eclipsed and others aren't, how we're still reading, en masse, about the great white whale and the scarlet letter, the boats borne ceaselessly back, the song of myself, the tolling bell, but not the vast majority of stories known and loved in the hour of their making. Horgan himself had been gone but a day when Richard Bernstein, writing the *New York Times* obituary, all but relegated the man to an infinitude of obscurity:

Still, despite much praise and commercial success, Mr. Horgan was commonly excluded from the lists of the foremost American writers of the century. Among the reasons given by critics who felt he belonged in the top rank were that his writing was too traditional and old-fashioned to compete with the likes of Faulkner or Hemingway; that he was seen primarily as a Catholic writer; that his writing, so concentrated on the Southwest, was too regional, and that he spread himself too thin over so many subjects and fields of interest.

Maybe? But Flannery O'Connor was Catholic. William Faulkner was regional. Ernest Hemingway was prolific. Wallace Stegner carried on sensationally in both nonfiction and fiction. And isn't style a matter of taste? Isn't "old fashioned" still being written and published and rightly acclaimed (see Jennifer Egan's *Manhattan Beach*, see Alice McDermott's everything) today?

In recent months I've been obsessed again with Horgan, with wanting, again, to understand. I've read for the first time his burnished recollections of his friend, Igor Stravinsky: "His hands were like exposed roots in winter, all gnarl and frosty fiber." I've read, again, that devastating kitten scene: "I could remember the hot thin supple body of the kitten under its wet fur, and the pitifully small tube of its neck, and the large clever space between its ears at the back, where all its thoughts seemed to come from, and the perfectly blank look on its wide-eyed face as it strove to escape me and the hurt I was possessed of."

I've turned to his craft book, *Approaches to Writing*, after writing my own—and been epigrammatically put in my place: "How can the negative ever create?" And "We begin to 'create' when we see everyone else as ourselves." And "Originality for its own sake is always dishonest and thus irrelevant." And "Every act of art is an act of love."

And I have driven, with my husband, from Pennsylvania to San Patricio, New Mexico, and sat outside in the coming dark in the company of Michael Hurd, Horgan's godson—yes, a man who did know Horgan.

Tell me about him, I said, and Michael pointed into the dusk, toward a black bird with white underwings, and spoke. Of Horgan's gentleness. Of Horgan's goodness. Of Horgan's equanimity. Of Horgan's devotion to chosen friends, ideals of truth, unfancy seeking, the quiet mysteries. Later Michael sent me a copy of a letter, addressed to him from Horgan, to whom Michael had sent examples of his art:

Well, dear Michael: I return your transparencies most grudgingly, for I shall miss them extremely–I've looked at them again and again, with the fullest delight and admiration. Your paintings in this group confirm most decisively what I've long felt–that you are a true painter, beautifully gifted, and your own man . . .

Surpassing generosity. You find it in Horgan's work. In the way the light streams out, away from the novelist and historian toward the perceived, and appreciated, landscape, person, thing. In the way the teacher in him yields all that he knows: "It is not possible to create the moderately good work without imagining the utmost great." In the way he catalogs the gifts of others—in monographs, in prefaces, in the profiles and essays he collected in *A Certain Climate* and *Tracings*, in his full-length autobiography-biography, *Encounters with Stravinsky*. In the letter he wrote to Michael—"with fullest delight and admiration"—and in the words David McCullough quotes in *A Writer's Eye: Field Notes and Watercolors by Paul Horgan*, words from Michael's mother, Henriette Wyeth Hurd: "His devotion is so warm and dazzling and profound. He is always giving. Most people don't, you know. People can be so pinched and cold. Paul is always giving."

Can generosity sustain itself? Is generosity legacy? Those, too, are questions. Might generosity be too fragile, too unreciprocated, too torqued with other-century civility? Might it be a night bloom, like the *cereus grandiflora* that features in *Everything to Live For* and opens "to achieve what no one there could do—to bloom into fulfillment without let or thought, and in opening to full life, neither give nor feel pain"?

Might literary generosity be a kind of grace that cannot redeem itself?

I don't know, but I know this: generosity is not finally fixed, ranked, or hallmarked. Generosity—in the prose on the page, in the life of the writer—calls upon us to notice. To send a letter. To write a postscript. To say: I see you. I thank you. You are not vanished here.

WHAT DOES IT MEAN TO
REVIEW A MEMOIR?

———

FIRST APPEARED IN *CHICAGO TRIBUNE*

REVIEWING. Could there be a more delicate matter? Open a book. Read the pages. Opine.

About another's ideas and fantasies. About another's obsessions and grammar. About another's particular and possibly peculiar way of seeing, wanting, dreaming. Here is a book. Now make it yours. Tell the world if it is good or bad. Give it a grade or a star or deny it a star. Put it on a "best of" list, or don't. Declare your response as if your response takes precedence over the book itself. As if your words about the book should be the book's final words.

The quickest route to understanding the many shady grays of the reviewing business is to publish a book of your own and to watch. I've read reviews of my books in which the critic (for better or worse) appears not to have read my book at all. I've read reviews that have made impossible assertions ("She introduces a main character in the last two pages." "She is at least 970 years old." "She doesn't know what love is.") I've read reviews that have been downright libelous and deliberately destructive, reviews that have been sprung from a not-so-private agenda, reviews designed to make headlines for the reviewer.

But no matter what the reviewer says, no matter how accurately or inaccurately the words reflect the book itself, those words stand. Countless more people will read the review of a book than the book itself.

Being reviewed is a game of roulette. Being a reviewer is something other. It's a responsibility, an opportunity, a chance to grow quiet and reflect. We review, or should review, not for our own gain, not to advance ourselves at the expense of the author, but to enter into a conversation, to explain, with as much care as we can summon, what it was like to spend time in the company of this author and this thing she's given birth to.

The job of a reviewer is to ask and to reveal: What is this story? What is its purpose? How was the story made? Does it feel true, is it original, does it come from a thoughtful place, and is it part of a tradition or does it break a mold? Is this book before this reviewer a mere platform or an urgent plea? Is it part of a brand or proof of a search? Has the author written to trumpet herself or to elevate a possibility? Have risks been taken? Will this story last?

Reviewers: these are our questions.

It's hard enough to wrangle with the reviews of books of fiction, politics, history, craft, but what of memoir? How do we fairly review those? These personal stories of failure and transcendence, wrong turns and right resolves, naked hearts and naked conditions? These remembrances shaped into stories? These survivor tales? How do we critique the personal without judging the person himself—the choices he's made, the badness he's confessed to, the need he has felt for ... something? Do we have any moral right to shame the author? Is it up to us to suggest that she needs a trip to rehab, or that she won't be invited, anytime soon, to our own kitchen table?

At the University of Pennsylvania, where I teach memoir, we sit side by side and elbow to elbow around an old rectangular table. We read one another's lives. We see one another's eyes. We have not come to judge how much he drinks, how much she hurts, how little she now speaks to her own mother. We don't engage in gossip.

Instead, we say to one another: Here is where I lived your story, and here is where I somehow couldn't. Here is where your present tense interferes with your search for wisdom. Here is where the story grows fussy, and here is where the lines grow fuzzy. Here is where the detail is neither clarifying nor seductive. And here is where you do not seem to fairly regard the others in your story. We say: What would happen if you told this story in second person, or began your prologue where the epilogue ends, or set aside this too-familiar theme in favor of another?

We say, is this, in fact, the right story to tell? Can you go bigger, can you go farther with memory and imagination?

We weigh matters of context, insularity, universality. We point to places where the voice is fierce and places where the scenes are skinny. We identify where the memoir makes room for the reader of the memoir. We ask what more might have been and what might have been done better. We put the work-in-progress down and return to books that teach us something — to *H is for Hawk* (Helen Macdonald), *Bettyville* (George Hodgman), *M Train* (Patti Smith), *Gabriel* (Edward Hirsch), *Can't We Talk About Something More Pleasant?* (Roz Chast). We reach out to one another so that we can all reach more deeply in.

Castigation plays no role in this. Guilt isn't the lesson. We are never better than the person beside us. We seek a best-told story.

Easy to do? Never. Essential? Yes. A set of guidelines applicable to books already published? I think so. Whether reviewing for an established journal or an online community, there is no excuse for the short cut, no room for easy cruelty, no gold stars for sarcasm or insults. Arrogance and superiority are sugar highs, at best. They do not advance the conversation.

A memoirist writes of the life she's lived. How she made her story art, if she made her story art, if she made her story matter not just to her but to the reader — those are the relevant facts of the matter.

We throw enough rocks at each other in this world. We fire far too many bullets, drop too many bombs, hurt without just cause. Reviewing becomes a warscape of its own when the reviewer of memoir chooses to forget that it is not the life itself we are asked to judge, but how that life has been swept up into words.

There is a difference.

THE MEMOIRS AND THE MEMOIRISTS

———

I WANT TO READ THE MEMOIRIST WHO IS UNEASY WITH EASE. THE ONE WHO DOUBLES BACK, ISN'T SURE, SCUFFS THE PAGE WITH MAYBE.

THE NARROW DOOR

PAUL LISICKY

The book was written across the span of a single year, and it wants to be a record of a mind wandering through some implicit, interrelated questions: what is friendship, what is attachment, who are we when we lose our dearest ones? I didn't want the book to feel chaotic, so I tried to organize each section around an image. One image talks to the next image and the next image and so on. So its structure is more associative than linear.
— Paul Lisicky

The Narrow Door is a devastating and devastatingly beautiful look at two treasured friendships in Lisicky's life—one with the writer Denise Gess and one with Lisicky's former husband, a man named M.

I seek the new in memoir. I believe that risks are well worth taking. In *Door*, Lisicky pursues a structure of slipped time and interweaves. We see Denise vibrant, we see M.'s charms, we see the turns these friendships will take, the toxic releases, the unspoken hurts, the flailed anger, the unstoppable rise of Lisicky's talent and the costs of that said talent. Denise is near death; she is alive again. M. and Lisicky are in love; the love is breaking; the love is new. Propelled forward. Slung straight back. The year is 2010, 2004, 2010, 2012, and does it matter, how these numbers fall? In between, the gnarly earth hurls lava up through volcano spouts, tsunamis speed toward shorelines, hurricanes smash into lives;

Joni Mitchell sings. The world may be so much bigger than one man's woes, Lisicky says. But also: the world speaks directly for and of them.

Here, for example, is Lisicky reflecting on that tsunami as he anticipates its deadly arrival. It's a certitude, happening worlds away. But it's also highly personal.

The speed of the wave has been compared to the speed of a jetliner, and perhaps that's what I find compelling about the phenomenon. But there is that impulse in us that says, come on, wave. Come on. Slop over car and grass and shrub: come on. The inevitable, this thing that wants to do us in: we can't watch the spectacle of it with any distance or detachment. We can't see that this wave is not about us.

By manipulating time, by seeing big and distant things as near, abrading intimacies, Lisicky, in *Door*, reminds the reader (and the memoir writer) that chronology is rarely the story.

Juxtapositions.Parallels. Metaphors.

Found meaning.

THE SOUL OF AN OCTOPUS

SY MONTGOMERY

All my books are, at heart, books about kindness/compassion, though occasionally exploring the consequences of its lack. One of the highest and best uses of writing, I would think, is to show kindness in action. I am lucky in that the individual animals I've written about seem to have been particularly gifted at bringing out the best in the people around them: Christopher Hogwood of The Good Good Pig *gave confidence to the girls next door, offered comfort to a dying teen, created a community of friends, and showed me how to be a better human. The octopuses I came to know and love at New England Aquarium gave all of us involved a way to share our best and most honest selves with one another, even when many of us were shy or on the autistic spectrum or facing family difficulties. The pink dolphins of yet another book, with their beauty and grace and mystery, drew from those who knew them best the inspiration for stories of connection and transformation.*
— Sy Montgomery

The Soul of an Octopus is Sy Montgomery as Sy Montgomery, which is to say the intrepid explorer with the gonzo heart. It's Montgomery spending Wonderful Wednesdays with her friends at the New England Aquarium as they get to know—and be known by—a succession of form-shifting, camouflage-bedazzling, big-one-minute-squeezing-through-a-two-inch-crevasse-the-next octopuses. She falls in love with the first octopus touch. She begins to live on octopus time. She scubas into seas to see the wild octopus up close. And then she returns to the barrels and tanks and public displays to watch Octavia and Kali and Karma conveyor-belt food up their suction cups toward their mouths, beat with three hearts, unlock puzzles, and demonstrate intelligence, compassion, and personality akin to any human being.

We can't help but love (even more) the wise and personality-prone octopus as we read (and finish) this book. We also can't help but love Montgomery, who embodies the kindness she seeks:

Perhaps, as we stroked her in the water, we entered into Athena's experience of time—liquid, slippery, and ancient, flowing at a different pace than any clock. I could stay here forever, filling my senses with Athena's strangeness and beauty, talking with my new friends.

LIFE WITHOUT A RECIPE

DIANA ABU-JABER

Life Without A Recipe *took forever to find its form. First I tried to be totally outline-ish. I was going to do it chronologically, knock it down one story at a time, each chapter interspersed with various findings about life or writing or the creative path. Then I kind of had to start over again. It kept morphing—writing lessons, kid stories, no chronology, alternating chapters. Then my lovely editor used the image of fashioning it like a flower, and my heart really sank because I had no idea what that meant, but I just kept pretending like I did and trying not to cry.*

At some point her excellent assistant got involved too and she did this sort of very strategic repositioning of various passages and chapters for me— I think they were also starting to worry about my mental state by this point and whether I was going to survive the revision process. Luckily, I knew I'd been blessed with editorial geniuses, so I just kept going. Gradually I began to understand that the structure kind of collapses time—it's organized according to a kind of emotional chronology. It was like rice paper origami, where you have to keep folding and folding and can't imagine what on earth it's going to look like, until the thing is done. It was kind of like that.
— Diana Abu-Jaber

Life Without a Recipe may sound like another foodie memoir, and in places it is. Meals get served. Cakes release steam. Lamb gets enhanced by garlic, snipped rosemary, pepper. Eggs meet with sugars.

But Diana Abu-Jaber's primary concern is nourishment—where we find it, how we take it, how we yield it. Her characters are her grandmother and her father, her wrong men and her right one, her little girl, and all the places Abu-Jaber has lived and traveled through. Her dialogue is elemental. She stares toward the stars and into the tantalizing goo of bowls and thinks about what it is to serve and to be served. Time is a koan. Family is young and old, near and gone.

Here Abu-Jaber is, in the very early pages, teaching her daughter to bake. A cracked egg floats in the bottom of a bowl. Gracie, her daughter, wants to know what an egg is, or does. "You started with an egg. Just a really teensy one," Abu-Jaber tells her.

"No I didn't," she says. She sounds distracted. Tilting the big ceramic bowl, she might be considering the beginning of life, the ends of the cosmos. The whorl at the center of the batter. A bowl is a place to find meaning, I think. Stir the spoon and wait, all sorts of things rise to the mind's surface. I used to joke that I wanted a child so I'd have someone to bake with. Perhaps not such a big joke.

One of the things I love about this book is its construction. It is a book built like a life, which is to say that it sets off down many roads; it encounters detours. Sometimes the stories get ahead of Abu-Jaber. Sometimes we watch her trying to get a hold of them:

Now, I sit outside at the café table with my notebook. I'll stay here and work until I can't see the ink. In the distance, bundled dark clouds move continents across the sky; far-off thunder murmurs in the ground, but up close a moth opens black wings, tumbling through the wind, playing, it seems, around the edges of the storm.

MY LIFE AS A FOREIGN COUNTRY

BRIAN TURNER

I initially began by writing, or attempting to write, a series of haibun, or variations on the haibun in English. After I'd reached about 90 pages or so, I sent them off to an editor that I was working with at the time (Ted Genoways) and boiled it all down into a 22-page essay called "My Life as a Foreign Country." Those 90 pages appeared mostly as fragments, and the fragmented approach seemed to me, in a psychological sense, to offer the best avenue into the meditation I was after—on war, violence, martial valor, memory, inheritance, and more.

Once I had this initial essay in hand, I realized that a book had announced itself and that I would need to lean into the much longer meditation available within a project of that magnitude. At first, I tried to write nine chapters (with a gesture to the nine muses), and I wrote a draft of the book that had nine chapters with completely different lenses and approaches. As a whole, they cycled through the meditative landscape that I was intrigued by, but they didn't satisfy the needs of a large-scale meditation. It was clunky and disjointed. And so, similar to the process with the first essay, I worked with another editor to isolate the necessary moments, to discover and keep the fragments that felt like doorways into knowledge—anything that held possibility, or glimpses of the profound, the sublime, the crucial.

I then separated all of the various fragments, as if unstitching Frankenstein to place like portions together. Visions of war and military service went into one pile. Family and inheritance into another.

Childhood. Mystery. Beauty. And so on. Once we had these basic groupings of fragments, we tried to create internal arcs—utilizing classic story structure theory at this point.

I think it's useful to think of these groups or piles of fragments as 'threads'—which we then braided together and placed and sometimes stretched throughout the sections of the book as it exists now.
— Brian Turner

Brian Turner's *My Life as a Foreign Country* tells us something of his sergeant years in Iraq, something of the wars his grandfather, father, and uncle fought. He slides in and out of what he remembers and what he conjures, sees the thoughts of a suicide bomber, sings the song of the bomb builder, looks beyond the enemy. His dreams are feral and his details are specific. Sometimes, even, our narrator is dead.

Turner's pages embrace many forms. The language smears and catches:

This is part of the intoxication, part of the pathology of it all. This is part of what I was learning, from early childhood on—that to journey into the wild spaces where profound questions are given a violent and inexorable response, that to travail through fire and return again—these are the experiences which determine the making of a man. To be a man, I would need to walk into the thunder and hail of a world stripped of its reason, just as others in my family had done before me. And if I were strong enough, and capable enough, and god-damned lucky enough, I might one day return clothed in an unshakable silence. Back to the world, as they say.

RIVERINE

_____

ANGELA PALM

*I focused on questions—small and large ones. Easily researched ones
and unanswerable ones. I also looked at connections, or the way dispa-
rate events and ideas seemed to be related, which led to more questions
and more revision. The symbols, as you say, sometimes formed the connective tissue I explored and I found those explorations intellectually
enjoyable. There were, luckily, enough questions surrounding the material in* Riverine *to propel that sustained urgency, which is such a wonderful and apt way to describe it. If there had been no motivation to
understand certain events, to peel back the layers of a place and time
to see how they worked in the way that a mechanic might take apart
an engine to isolate particular parts, I might have lost steam. But because certain things are irreversible and certain answers unavailable,
the writer then must come to value the pursuit of truth (the questions)
as much as truth itself (the answers)—value taking the engine apart as
much as putting it back together and making it run.*

*When I found myself muddled in some difficult impasse in the writing,
I often turned to a favorite passage of Bret Lott's that goes like this:
"The form known as creative nonfiction is something akin to Russian
nesting dolls, one person inside another inside another. But instead of
finding smaller selves inside the self, the opposite occurs: we find nest-
ed inside that smallest of selves a larger self, and a larger inside that,
until we come to the whole of humanity within our own hearts." This
reminded me that the only way to access the universal was through*

the personal, and it gave me reason to keep going back to the page (or screen, as it were).

Writing about one's own experiences and the hard truth of them can begin to feel like fable. Once you tell a story about yourself, it becomes just that, a story, which is a cultural dimension that is both separate from and connected to experience. When we tell the stories of our lives, it is possible and even natural, I think, to first cast ourselves and others in familiar roles. The boy in the window easily becomes the quintessential bad boy, the forbidden love interest, the villain, and even the knight in shining armor. Heroes emerge, and supporting characters do their bit. And to avoid those easy classifications, and thus make the personal interesting to anyone other than oneself, one must tell more stories. I ask myself, after much is already put to paper, what is the most interesting thing about this experience? What other knowledge do I possess or can I acquire that informs this story in a meaningful way? What is this really about and why should anyone care?
— Angela Palm

Angela Palm is an exceptional writer. A burst-onto-the-scene sort whose first book, *Riverine,* won the Graywolf Press Nonfiction Prize.

I fall hopelessly in love with risk-taking writers. Palm takes mighty risks. Her metaphors are perpetually expanding. Her ideas whirl with tornado force. She elevates the art of the motif. She is obsessed with land, river, a boy. She lives and examines unconventional choices. She breaks free of childhood landscapes only to return to all she's left behind. The stuff and story of it.

Throughout the book, Palm asserts the power of juxtaposition and her willingness to subscribe, to a young mind, the abundant wisdoms of a backward-gazing adult. Palm's divagations most frequently twine back to a boy named Corey, her next-door neighbor, who returns, in scene after scene, as a child in a window, a glimpse of the future, the choice Palm ultimately cannot make when an act of irredeemable, uncharacteristic violence sends Corey to prison for life.

Palm writes like this:

At points in my life, I would keep choosing trees over people. I would keep escaping through the boughs of pines, sap-handed and daydreaming. Higher and higher, as if some kind of answer lay waiting at the upper limit of the world. Meditation would become a way out, a quicker exit to the sky, a way to soften a seized heart, a way of remembering what the mind can do.

And this:

Time is change, more than a beginning and an end, but an ongoing expansion. One thing can become another—gradually, and then suddenly, as Ernest Hemingway once said. And cheese is part art and part nature. I have seen that and more. Writing is seeing, there is an obligation to complete the half-written letters, assemble the tales, stitch together the truths. Of that, I am certain.

In *Riverine*, one is reminded of Mary Karr (*The Liars' Club*) as Palm reports on her father and the men who gather for games of card, who laugh "their gravelly laughs," who take "another drink from their cans of beer," and who allow the observant Palm into their circle. One returns, in one's mind, to J.R. Moehringer's *The Tender Bar*, as Palm describes her years working at the local dive, the River, which, with its sad stories and deep connections, becomes, to her, "another kind of church." One also thinks, when reading Palm, of Annie Dillard and Dillard's saturated metaphors— Dillard's inclination to see, in natural things, the portent of human choice and consequence. Palm does that, too. Often. From the chapter titled "Bifurcation": "Above us, a silver moon hung sideways from a black sky. Soon, the world would swing sideways with it, unhinged, split wide and dripping."

THEN WINTER

CHLOE HONUM

I wanted to draw readers deeply into the sometimes unsettling world of the collection, and I found the prose poem form to be inviting in its sturdiness and familiarity. At the same time, the unbroken lines allowed me a kind of release into imagination. I found that the form lends itself to both scene and surrealism somehow, perhaps in the way the sentences surge forward. That sense, and my draw to prose poems in the first place, was certainly influenced by Mark Strand, whose beautifully surreal prose poems I was reading at the time of writing Then Winter.

In writing these poems, I felt a longing for clarity. The speaker is going through a time of intense inner turmoil and is trying to reattach herself to the world. While I wanted to stay true to the wildness of that experience, in terms of syntax and imagery, I craved precision. Naming things clearly, where possible, felt essential to bringing the new terrain into focus. White space, then, became an important tool. Poems are made of both language and silence, and white space, both in and around poems, can help create room for the distilled image or moment to come through.
— Chloe Honum

Chloe Honum's near-perfect chapbook, *Then Winter*, offers meditations and stories about a psychiatric ward. The book is pristine, but beneath the quiet, fractures lurk. There are the persistent fluorescent lights, the softening of winter, the ravages of a war a man carries forward. There is what the speaker misses, and there is the big leap of hope.

Once, in an interview, Honum said that "lyric poetry has a way of taking my guard down. I'm listening to music, absorbing the imagery, not concerning myself with logical reactions, and meanwhile the poem is carving a deep path." In much of *Then Winter* Honum forsakes the cutting of poetry into lines for the continuous run of a prose poem. The choice is deeply affecting, making the collection read like a single cohering story.

IMAGINE WANTING ONLY THIS

―――――

KRISTEN RADTKE

I prioritize images when immediacy or speed is important. A clean illustration can convey in an instant what might take a paragraph in prose. That's not to say I find images superior, or more effective than words—just that they function differently in terms of how a reader or viewer receives and engages with them. In drawings, too, I might include a lot of visual information that I'd never describe in prose because it's unnecessary to the argument or plot—like the objects on a nightstand, for example, in a drawing of a character getting out of bed. A reader can choose whether or not they want to engage with that part of the drawing, and it can be present to create a fuller portrait without slowing down the narrative.
— Kristen Radtke

"WE FORGET that everything will become no longer ours," Kristen Radtke writes in *Imagine Wanting Only This,* one of the most haunting graphic memoirs I've ever held in my hands.

Radtke, at this stage in her story, is touring ruins. She has reflected on ruin lust and ruin value and ruin porn. She has visited Corregidor and Siquijor, the empty streets of Burma, the killing fields of Cambodia, Laos, "calcifying" cities. She has forsaken and been forsaken, she is audacious and vulnerable, she is wounded by how it bends back upon itself, and as we turn the pages on her journey, we are ravaged and ravished.

There is a proud tradition of graphic memoirists—of those dually equipped to wield word and image to tell the true and deeply considered story of a life. Alison Bechdel, Roz Chast, Riad Sattouf, David Small, Art Spiegelman, and others have done it searingly well. Add now to that list Kristen Radtke, who proves herself an equal among equals with this debut book.

Radtke begins her story with memories of a loved uncle, her "favorite person that I knew in real life," who, in a breathtaking series of wordless panels, introduces the young girl to the possibility of magic and the yellow flight of fireflies. This uncle will die in time, as other members of the family have, of an inherited heart condition. Radtke herself will not escape these genes. She's just nineteen, when she understands that her body has also been implicated.

Chapter 1, following the prologue, finds Radtke setting out for Gary, Indiana, with her college boyfriend, Andrew. Gary was once called the "City of the Century," but it is now broken panes and stuck locks, a home to an abandoned cathedral where, as Radtke writes, "Ivy overtook the corroding walls as it does in storybooks, covering the slated stone with spindles of earthy webs." And: "The tarnished pedals of a shattered organ lay in the corner, its broken keys like piles of pulled teeth."

Within this rubble, Radtke will find "mold-smeared photographs," which she will take as her own, the stuff of an art installation she spontaneously decides that she will (someday) make.

But, as Radtke will soon discover, the images she has taken were no random bits of trash. They belonged, in fact, to a young ruins-obsessed photographer who had been struck dead days before by a train, and they had been placed among all that glorious rot by his friends; they had been sprinkled with his ashes. What is it that Radtke has stolen? What belongs to anyone, ever and especially when a place seems to have lost its purpose, or had its purpose rearranged by time?

THE WRONG WAY
TO SAVE YOUR LIFE

MEGAN STIELSTRA

A few years back I had a piece in The Best American Essays, *about healing from postpartum depression by stalking my neighbor via a wireless video baby monitor. I wrote it on a fellowship to Ragdale, a residency program in Illinois. Then I read a messy draft at an event for mothers at my kid's elementary school. Then I performed it for 2nd Story where I had a curator, a theater director, a sound designer, and a live audience. Then it was published by Roxane Gay at* The Rumpus, *and I started getting emails from women in the thick of it and the men and women who love them and were trying to understand. Then it was selected by Cheryl Strayed for* Best American Essays, *and I got more emails. A lot more of them. Then I recorded it for Radio National Australia, then NPR, and I was interviewed about it at all sorts of places, and it was reprinted in the UK, and I saw it passed around on Twitter by postpartum support centers, and now it's being made into a short film.*

And people helped me. They held my hand while I cried, and took care of my son so I could—first—find my way back to myself and—then, slowly—carve out time to remember how to write. I have a partner who is fully involved in raising our son. I had, at the time, health insurance, which is such a huge factor in a writer's ability to produce. My students lit a fire under my ass and I tried my best to return the favor. My boss (at my day job in faculty development) believed in my writing. Ragdale (thank you, Ragdale) gave me desperately needed time. The mothers at my kids' school let me know that piece had value. The live audience laughed and cried; I could hear how the story worked and where I could improve it. Roxane believed in me. Cheryl believed in me. I aspire to be as supportive and generous as these two women; they've taught me that, as doors open, we turn around and say, okay, everybody, let's go. Above all else, that essay traveled because of the women on the other end of its pages, all of us together in the fog and the mess and shit. I was never alone, not in the living of the experience and not in the writing of the experience, and if any of those women are reading this now, please know that I see you. Please know how grateful I am that you reached out. Here I am, reaching back.

Real talk: that accolade made things happen for me. Book, publications, agent, new book, bigger advance, more time to write. I want to be transparent about this because I think it's important to talk about what success means; who gets to have it, who doesn't, whose voices are missing. I want to be worthy of it. I want to use my growing platform in a way that supports writers who, as Richard Wright wrote, "make the world look different:" Specifically, women's voices. Specifically, women of color. Specifically, queer men and women, trans men and women, gender fluid and nonconforming. Specifically, international perspectives, class perspectives, perspectives that challenge me to look past my own. We need a democratization of publishing that allows us to get closer to what it means to be a human being in this world.
— Megan Steilstra

Megan Stielstra is (at the same time) a fiercely intelligent writer and an ultra hip one. In my *Chicago Tribune* review of *Once I Was Cool*, I (emphatically) declared:

Stielstra's prose is appraising, luck counting, educational, if we can agree that "educational" is a sexy word. [Educational is a sexy word.] She is a

Kafka scholar, a performance artist, a multi-tasker, a woman who writes her stories while sitting on the bathroom floor as her toddler sings invitations for play. She's the kind of mom who shows up at the school events not with the baked goods but the juice—and feels bad enough to tell the tale. She is a fan of the essay, but not the kind that gets typically taught. She is a writing teacher and a writing appreciator; for us (and only for us) she has assembled a list of things that must be read. She likes footnotes, she wields footnotes, she succeeds with footnotes. She is funny, she is tough, her Dad taught her guns, her mom taught her books, and she's not even going to try to pretend not to be head over heels for her super tall husband and her superhero son.

Stielstra is that same writer all over again in *The Wrong Way to Save Your Life*, a collection of essays organized around the decades of her living. In pieces about her father's health, the complexities of love, taking a stand, the astonishment of motherhood, and the act of writing, she mostly invites us to reflect on our own fears.

"We have to look at that fear," she writes. "We have to get into it. Throw it against the wall, stand back and take a good close look. It's ugly: heavy, dark, and centuries in the making. You might want to move on, to turn it off, watch something else, but wait—look again."

THE BOOK OF SEPARATION

TOVA MIRVIS

I wrestled with the structure constantly. For years, my head was filled with arcs and intersecting lines.

The present tense was one arc: the year of leaving, spanning from one September to the next September, from one Jewish New Year to the next. This arc is told in the present tense, and the fact that it was a specified year helped me create a clear structure and sense of time that grounds the reader in the narrative movement of the book. I made sure the reader knew where we were in that year, looking for markers to keep the reader oriented in time. This felt especially important because the book is a story of change over time and I needed the reader to be aware of that passage of time.

But other parts of the story beyond the year of leaving needed to be told as well and this created a more complicated arc. There was the far past: growing up in the Orthodox world, getting married, having kids, and eventually realizing that I was not going to stay. This backstory, which I did want to lay out chronologically, needed to be spliced into the present story, unfolding with its own smaller arc, its own tension and pacing: an arc within an arc. But the far past also needed to intersect with the present story in a way that was thematically consistent and resonant. And making it more complicated was what I called "the near past." I couldn't wait until the end of the book (when the chronology of the far past arrived closer to the present-day arc) to relay to the reader important details about my marriage and my religious feelings. So I needed to work in these more recent past events where they were needed to flesh out the present day story.

I constantly reshuffled the way the past intersects the present. Should I alternate chapters past and present? Have big chunks of past as separate sections? Have minimal backstory because it was too hard to splice it in without interrupting the narrative flow? In our minds, of course we move constantly between past and present—but on the page, it's harder because we don't want a reader to get confused, we don't want to lose forward momentum, or make the narrative feel choppy, or have the reader ask: why am I being told this now? I wanted those detours into the past to feel seamless, but trying to create an illusion of seamlessness is very labor-intensive.

I wrote out the different events I wanted to cover on note cards that I spread across my living room floor, forming the different arcs. I looked for moments of thematic intersection—to spot an opening in the present story where the past could be folded inside. Some came easily and some were hard to find. I felt as though I was working a large puzzle, needing to see the structure in a physical way, on the floor, before I could see it on the page. (Do NOT walk in the living room! I warned my kids.)

Eventually, when I found those openings and spliced the past into the present, I felt like I was a tour guide leading a group along uncertain terrain and telling them: We're taking a detour now, but trust me, I know why we're going here now and I promise I will get you back on the path soon.
— Tova Mirvis

The Book of Separation is a brave, bold book that takes us straight into the mind of a woman raised to embrace a faith and way of living that does not, ultimately, fit. Its author, Tova Mirvis, is a writer and a seeker, a mother of three loved children, a wife. She has observed the rules of her Orthodox-Jewish faith—covered her hair, slept in separate marital beds when biology dictates, abided distinctions and rituals. Forty, now, she wonders what might happen if she actually chose the framing of her life. If she lived according to the instincts that percolate within.

Or might percolate. If only she was graced the chance to find out.

Leaving a faith, in this case, means leaving a family. It means striking out where few have gone, writing the stories she seeks to write, loving a new man who gives her light, repairing the curls on her own head. It means answering the questions her children have about once forsaken pizzas and Halloweens and being together. It means driving highways to unknown destinations, eating granola bars on holy days, and recalibrating traditions.

"Leaving isn't just about engaging in a set of once-forbidden actions," Mirvis writes. "It's about changing the family story. Orthodoxy has always been my home, and to leave it is to leave home as well."

Later: "Love is what you risked losing if you wanted to choose for yourself."

And: "Orthodoxy was the life he wanted and the truths in which he believed. If you believed in those rules, you had a life built of tradition and ritual, richly populated with family and community. But if you didn't believe, then those same structures could be a prison. You could stay by carving out private spaces for yourself, but even then, you always had to be aware of the gap between who you were and who you were supposed to be."

GUIDEBOOK TO RELATIVE STRANGERS

———

CAMILLE T. DUNGY

When the conversation explored in "The Conscientious Outsider" first happened, I was indignant. But I don't suppose a reader would care to dwell too long in a narrative that is solely an account of one person's frustration with another individual. I had to express clear insights about what exactly made the conversation so awkward and painful. Not just the what but also the why and the how and the why it matters. The essay develops context and history, and it also formulates actionable means toward positive change. This is what good writing can do—perhaps must do. It's not just a matter of pointing to something and saying, "I experienced an experience that hurt." I want to invite readers into the context of that experience in such a way that their own bodies and minds enter the moment as well. Furthermore, I write toward discovering ways forward. That's, I suppose, one of the differences between anecdote and essay. The essay plumbs the anecdote more deeply. I invite readers to move beyond their own quick reactions and learn to feel and understand alongside me.
— Camille T. Dungy

Now and then my first editor, Alane Mason of W.W. Norton, will send me a book that she thinks I'll like. *A gift from Alane*, I'll think. This time the book was *Guidebook to Relative Strangers: Journeys into Race, Motherhood, and History* by the poet and essayist Camille T. Dungy.

Alane publishes necessary books. This book is necessary. A collection of essays about a traveling poet-lecturer who, in journeying across the country with her young daughter, becomes, in the words of the flap copy, "intensely aware of how they are seen, not just as mother and child, but as black women."

There are motherhood stories here. Stories of outrage. Stories of community and history.

AMONG THE LIVING AND THE DEAD: A TALE OF EXILE AND HOMECOMING ON THE WAR ROADS OF EUROPE

INARA VERZEMNIEKS

Having come from a family of refugees, and having only ever known my family as one that had been divided and scattered by war, I felt such an intense desire whenever I was in Latvia to just be with my family, to take in what it felt like to be part of something whole, to experience what it was like to just live—together, as a family lives together. There was something so deeply satisfying helping with the daily chores, picking beetles off the potatoes, canning, foraging in the forest. My relatives were always saying, you can go write, it's OK. *But to me, that was part of the writing, feeling this in my bones, rather than theoretically, from a distance. I can see now that it also served another important purpose: because of the trauma in my life, like so many who have found a way forward through such experiences, I became very good at disassociating, observing from the edges, regarding things with a kind of intense detachment.*

I suspect it's why reporting felt like such a home for me. But for this book, something so personal, I had to learn a knew way of approaching my work, one that required me to literally place myself inside the narrative, to commit to being present, a presence. I remember showing an old editor and mentor an early draft and he said, the longer you are in the landscape, the more you, as a narrator, begin to physically manifest as a character. *And that was how it felt: the longer I was in Latvia, the more connected to myself I felt. I was so strong after those visits—stronger than I've ever felt. I'd run every morning through wheat fields. I'd found new muscles from all the picking and hoeing and cutting. My hands and feet were calloused. I also made it a point to be there for the different seasons, because life in the Latvian countryside is so tied to the rhythms of the weather. The winters, especially, are hard and long and dark. And I felt different inside that, too: more alert inside the stillness, slower, more cautious.*

All those things came to influence the writing, I think, by giving me not just facts, but new ways of feeling, of perceiving, to transmit through words.
— Inara Verzemnieks

Among the Living and the Dead is a memoir of history and home, of dispersal and return, of Latvia and love. It is one extended prose poem, a book of magnificent reach and heart. Verzemnieks is deeply engaged with the stories she was told when she was young. She is deeply engaged with the stories she finds in history books and documents warehoused in foreign places. The book is rich, as well, with the physical, as the author travels across thousands of miles, walks through forests, tends farms, immerses herself in a scalding sauna, smudges the grime away from a framed photograph, encounters a sharp-toothed dog, and sits at a table eating foreign things.

The Latvians have a saying, she tells us: "I feel along with you." The saying prompts her to reflect, "As if any true act of empathy demands not only emotional projection but also physical accompaniment, a willingness to travel with the other, deep into the unknown of wherever it is they must go." That line alone is worth the price of the book.

BORDER SONGS

———

DAN SIMPSON AND ONA GRITZ

What I had at my disposal was pretty typical of the times in which I passed my formative years, the 1950s and '60s. From the age of three, when my identical twin brother Dave and I learned to operate a record player, I loved records—the Golden Records with songs and stories for children, yes, but also the old 78s our father had hanging around the house. I know now that some of the lyrics I heard couldn't have stood on their own, but being cloaked in music, they came with a beat and with a sense of line, and that was enough to hook me. One record Dave and I couldn't get enough of was "The Mocking Bird" by The Four Lads. That record disappeared long ago, but thanks to the wonders of the internet and all the people who put everything up there, I recently rediscovered it, and it still has that magic.

Speaking of magic, we had a copy of Frank Sinatra singing "That Old Black Magic." Even though I was too young to really understand what romance and passion were all about, I got a sense of the allure and danger they carried.

Our parents read to us, from nursery rhymes to poems like "The Owl and the Pussy Cat" and "Winkin', Blinkin', and Nod." I loved the sing-song rhythm and the surprise of a good rhyme, but here was something so visceral: that chill up and down the spine, the dropping of the elevator, and spinning like a ship caught in the tide, all happening at once.
— Dan Simpson

When I write a poem, or I should say, when I'm at my best while writing a poem, I'm feeling my way towards something—a connection, an understanding, a leap in logic. If I think I know exactly where I'm headed when I sit down to work, it's much more likely that the poem will sputter, stall, and end up going nowhere. It's as though I have to turn off my intellect and trust something much more internal and intuitive. When I'm fortunate enough to come to that place of completion and satisfaction you mention, it nearly always comes as a surprise to me. I actually catch myself wanting to look over my shoulder to see who it was that knew what I didn't about that moment or memory or encounter I'd been writing about. It can feel that separate. There's me with my limited ability to understand where I'm headed as I add words and images to the page, and then there's this other, wiser self who sees connective tissue and layers of meaning and can show me what the poem ultimately has to say.

I experience balance as a need to untangle the knots in my own understanding and to make some kind of sense out of lived experience with all its contractions and, yes, imbalance. I grew up in a household where big secrets were kept. My mother had an early marriage my sister and I didn't know about until we were teenagers. We had half-siblings we'd always thought were distant cousins. Our parents were both ten years older than we'd been told. Before these truths were revealed, there had always been holes in our family stories, gaps in logic, slips and hints that were hastily brushed aside. Something was off but I couldn't name it.

When I was very small I thought there was a secret room in our house. I pictured it filled with treasures—old dolls with beautiful porcelain faces, a wooden rocking horse with a thick, ropey mane. Part of me was aware that this room was imaginary, but another part understood that there was something actual hidden within our very walls. That instinct I had, that knowing without knowing exactly what it was I knew, is the voice I listen for when I sit down to write. It's the part of me that senses something going on beneath the surface and that recognizes imagination as one sure pathway to truth.

The best way I have found to access that voice when I sit down to write is to begin by reading. Among the many poets I find myself reaching for again and again are Sharon Olds who I read for courage and permission, Stephen Dunn for genuine and unconventional wisdom, and Linda Pastan for that quality we've been talking about of completion and surprise.
— Ona Gritz

One Christmas Eve—aloft in a high pew—I looked down upon the holiday crowd and found, to my delighted surprise, Dan Simpson and Ona Gritz, two people in love. Two people who, together, are far more than any single whole.

Ona Gritz has written of their beautiful partnership in a much-shared *New York Times* essay, "Love, Eventually." Simpson has written about his life—and the loss of his twin brother and best friend, Dave—in "Inside the Invisible: A Blind Writer's View of Living the Attentive Life." Both have written of their worlds in poems, and *Border Songs,* their chapbook, offers words to and for and across one another. It seams the years before they met. It declares their reach. It separately (but not really separately) considers biblical themes, John Lennon, and rainstorms.

I use the book to teach memoir. I use it to learn the art of extension and embrace.

FISHERMAN'S BLUES: A WEST AFRICAN COMMUNITY AT SEA

ANNA BADKHEN

There exists a very delicate line between withholding and oversharing, and it is a line I am very hesitant to approach. Modern Anglophone literature—and I am wielding the term "modern" broadly, to encompass the last hundred years, during which confessional literature became a thing—has produced and continues to produce a lot of trespass. I recognize that the sense of trespass is internal, and deeply subjective. Which is how oversharing happens. We live at a time of low bars.

I write to learn about what interests me, what I am curious about. Which means that by the mere fact of publishing my work I am already inviting you on a subjectively chosen, private journey. I am allowing you to see me in every word I choose, in every line I write.

At the same time, broadly speaking, what interests me is decidedly not me—I am curious about my human neighbors, in the planetary sense. So the reason I allow you to see me is to put in context, for you, my curiosities and my philosophical inquiries at the time of research and writing of this particular book. Fisherman's Blues is a book about boundaries because boundaries are, were, what was interesting to me about human nature at the time of my research and writing. Since I am your guide and your narrator, it is incumbent upon me to contextualize myself to you—enough so that you know why I pay attention to one thing and not the other. At this time.

Which begs the legitimate question: what is enough? I don't know.

And still it is up to me to make that decision. My instinct is to err on the side of less. (My beloved editor, Becky Saletan, gently corrects me toward more.) Yet even in this my decision you, the reader, will see me. Every choice I make on the page is me showing you who I am.
— Anna Badkhen

Magical nonfiction. It's a term that Anna Badkhen has used to describe the books she writes about the worlds she slides into and through. Northern Afghanistan. The African Savannah. The Senegalese port of Joal. These places have existed long without her. They are eternal, yet they are changing. They are her vessel and she is theirs. The residuals of those places live in her words.

In the case of *Fisherman's Blues*, Badkhen lives in a room rented from a retired fisherman. Its roof leaks. Its alley floods. Her pillow smells like rotten fish. The toilet is a pit. Outside, sometimes, a girl dances to cell phone music between dragging buckets of slop to the sea. By the port, women wait for the men who have set out in their pirogues to return from whatever the luminescent sea will give. But the sea gives less and less. The tides cannot be tamed.

There is a pirogue now that has Badkhen's name on it. There are people who won't forget the slender white woman with the notebook and the wherewithal to build a boat, to untangle nets, to draw the bloody fish in. The woman who swung from ropes as a child would. The woman who watches other women wait. The woman who writes, "In stories, as at sea, boundaries are malleable, begetters and destroyers both. The genii who marry humans cross a permeable membrane between the sacred and the everyday. Like storytellers, I think: We have the power of making magic real by how we engage it, by which stories we choose to tell. Or maybe the stories choose us."

AREAS OF FOG

WILL DOWD

Art is whatever you can get away with, and in Areas of Fog, *I let myself get away with a lot. I wrote prose poems, travel pieces, meditations, jokes. Each week I shifted tonally and formally according to pure creative whim. If the pieces hang together like clothes on a wash line, it's thanks (as you've noted) to the common theme, to the meteorological through line. It let me improvise. It let me sit down each Sunday morning and just start folding the paper like a rogue origamist, trusting that in the end something compelling would take shape. It gave me complete free reign.*

Well, almost complete free reign. Besides opening each entry with the weather, I did have one additional constraint, one unbreakable dictate: I had to write something. Every week. No exceptions.
— Will Dowd

Areas of Fog is a synthetic—the very best sort. Dowd is a poet and one might classify this book as prose poetry. But other things are also afoot as Dowd sets out to write, each week, about weather and its antecedents.

The book contains ephemera—the unbearable sun on the day Van Gogh was buried; Bach hating nice weather, for it cut into his commissions for funeral masses; Audubon and his Indian summer. It achieves a unity of theme while not existing as a ruinously uniform series of essays. Dowd messes with us. He teases us. He laughs at himself. He allows beauty.

SECOND SHIFT

SUSAN TEKULVE

Our mothers are our first earths, our first storytellers, so it's accurate to say that while my mom was dying of Alzheimer's dementia it often felt like the earth had shifted out from beneath me, and I couldn't make narrative sense out of what was happening to her. Still, for a long time I tried to explore the experience of losing her to this illness by writing in traditional narrative forms, which, typically, fizzled into long lists of her symptoms, or a series of disconnected images and sketches that I now refer to as "that 300-page hot mess." It wasn't until last spring, while my mother was in the late stages of the illness, that I realized I needed the constraints of the lyric. I wrote "Winter's Work" first as a lyric prose poem, and eventually it became a lyric flash essay.

In an interview, the poet Ellen Bryant Voigt defines the lyric as "born, perhaps, from recognition of impermanence, rather the opposite of chiseling a poem into stone—and unlike the chisel, it allows faster, multiple shifts of tone, redirections, mid-course corrections." What this means is that the lyric counters the structures of the sequential and linear often associated with the narrative. By taking on the lyric mode, I was able to juxtapose images, leap through metaphors, and use other lyric patterns to focus on a structural arrangement that de-emphasizes narrative sequence. By highlighting the lyric present, I found the moment of heightened emotional response and understanding that the essay explored.

Though I wasn't thinking about this at the time, I realize in retrospect that those lyric devices in the essay mirror the nonsequential narrative pathways in the mind of an Alzheimer's patient. My father, brother, and I had to follow these pathways while we tended my mother through all the stages of this disease. We had to respond quickly to abrupt shifts in her moods and abilities. We made a lot of mid-course corrections. Despite the long and lingering reminders of impermanence, my father, her primary caregiver, tended her all the way through. There were a number of times when I wondered whether my mother were still here at all, times when she felt entirely gone from me. I don't think my father ever lost track of her. All he said about the subject was, "Sixty years is a long time to be married. This is my job now." It's this kind of work, the kind that serves as devotion, that became the revelation of the essay.
— Susan Tekulve

In her new collection of essays, *Second Shift*, Susan Tekulve does many things extraordinarily well. She follows the trail of her own writerly beginnings. She takes us into the peril of a quiet neighborhood. She travels far away and comes back, worries for her husband and her son, and records the life of the family she knows and the neighbor whose life she had only guessed about.

The final essay in the book is a stunner—a handful of words about the slow vanishing of her mother. It is, in fact, a master class on form and lyric.

THE BEGINNING OF EVERYTHING

———

ANDREA BUCHANAN

So in writing about this "lost" time, this time when I was lost to myself, I had to do a bit of detective work. I searched through my gmail account and gathered all the emails I'd written between March 2015 and January 2017. I went through the notes I'd written on the Notes app on my phone. I went through text messages I'd saved and scoured the conversations about my health and what I was feeling. And I went through my medical records, noting dates and physician summaries and descriptions and medical jargon, and collating those with my own fleeting reflections from that time. In this way, I was able to recreate a timeline for myself, and find my way in to that period in which I had felt I wasn't fully there the first time around.

I used to make it very easy for myself to draw from and elucidate upon the events of my own life, as I was an avid journal-keeper. I have boxes and boxes of old notebooks and diaries, and files upon files of digital notes, most of which have no purpose outside of being a lurking potential source of embarrassment (or amusement, depending upon who's doing the reading). I had a trail to follow of the events of my life, sometimes written in real time as they unfolded, a breathless blow-by-blow, transcribed in real time. But when I was grappling with my spinal CSF leak, that trail ran cold. I didn't have the capacity to write and reflect, or to process in words on a page the things that were happening in my life. I was mute, for a time, my thoughts suspended in the silence of laying flat in my bed, every-

thing crowded out by pain. But every so often, I would rally: I would send a group email to my family and friends after doctors' appointments to update them on what was happening; in the rare moments after a procedure that gave my brain a bit of buoyancy, I would jot things down, or tap out notes on my phone; during a few courses of steroids I seized upon my increased energy as a chance to write down some of the things that had been floating in my mind.
— Andrea Buchanan

"Andrea Buchanan lost her mind while crossing the street one blustery March morning," the flap copy begins.

Wait, you say. *What?* Because this is no metaphor, as it turns out. Because, in fact, a terrible coughing spell had left a tiny hole in the *dura mater* of Buchanan's nervous system and her cerebrospinal fluid was leaking.

The Beginning of Everything tells this story—a story, in so many ways, about lost time and about the process of reassembling the facts of a life that a tiny membrane tear had so radically redefined.

"BUILDING A STRAW-BALE HOUSE—AND A NEW LIFE—AMONG CENTRAL OTAGO'S HILLS"

JILLIAN SULLIVAN

I began writing without a beginning—or several beginnings, not settling, but getting things down, writing my way toward what I wanted to capture and discover. A lot of it wasn't good enough to include. I knew that because I was bored writing it, and I said to myself, it's all right, just keep going. When I got lost I came back to my list of intentions.

I had random paragraphs, which I was at first worried about. I decided they would be my structure—like building a house of straw bales—one then another then another, and they would all tie in. But how? What would be the overarching structure that would hold it? I decided that place and weather, the sense of land and sky, was bigger than my own story, and would hold my story within it.

The intentions I set at the beginning: word count, structure, topic, what I hoped to discover, what I wanted to evoke for the reader, what I wanted to give to the reader. A mixture of grand ideas and specifics. Writing an intention at the beginning is like having a recipe to guide me.
— Jillian Sullivan

Jillian Sullivan is a New Zealander who writes fiction and nonfiction for all ages—and who built herself a straw-bale house.

She begins the essay "Building a Straw-Bale House" with a late autumn and a "once again" and a need for firewood that was gathered in summer—as well as a hearkening of the winter to come. Nearly all of the seasons appear, in other words, in a single paragraph, and yet Sullivan moves us easily through the seasons.

That's one magic trick in the essay. Another is the way that Sullivan sets Kingsolver, Vitruvius, and Joseph Campbell down alongside place names like Ida Burn and Hawkdun Mountain—without ever trying to explain who they are. It's a stellar act of intimacy—of a writer trusting the reader.

Finally, Sullivan is the voice of this essay, but she is also one among any—grandmothers, grandchildren, locals, the curious, and lost friends. She's written community straight into her work—and modeled it.

ALL YOU CAN EVER KNOW

————

NICOLE CHUNG

I wanted this story to answer two primary questions: What is it like to grow up Korean in a white family, without knowing the truth of your origins? And what happens when you attempt to find your missing past? Of course, from these big questions a host of others branch off, but these are the ones I began with. I wanted this book to be both question and answer, those two parts in dialogue, eventually coming together to reveal certain hard-won truths (but not necessarily a perfect, tidy resolution, because of course that rarely exists in real life). I wanted it to have space for all of my questions, and all the readers' as well.

Once I told this story chronologically, beginning with my childhood growing up adopted. After the book sold, I actually wrote a first full draft in which the plot largely unspooled in chronological order. I don't know why I did that. Maybe that was what I had to do to get all the parts down. It was fine, technically, but when I read it, the pacing felt off to me. The stakes were evident, but not quite coming across in an urgent way I was sure a reader needed to feel, too. The question of whether I'd ever know more—whether I'd search for my birth family, and then what that search would involve—needed to be asked, and answered, closer to the start. I decided I had to toggle back and forth between past and future; between moments from childhood, when maybe I'd had a particular question but not its answer, and moments in adulthood when I could finally go looking for those answers. I had to utilize that agitating backward glance you mention alongside my pursuit of my story.

So I spent a few weeks taking the whole book apart, scooting segments around, rewriting when necessary, moving back and forth in time. I wanted the past and the present sections, the wondering and the searching sections, to ask and answer each other's questions; to be in conversation. And then, due to all the time-jumping, particularly in the first half, it felt strange to break it into numbered chapters—even having numbers felt like imposing a kind of structure that didn't seem to fit the book anymore—so I divided the book into four parts instead. In the final version there are a lot of breaks that I suppose function like chapter breaks, but when I read it now I think of each of the four parts as its own long chapter. It's certainly not the form I would have imagined when I started writing, but it's what I ended up with in revision, and ultimately I think I settled on it just because it felt right.
— Nicole Chung

In memoir, plot can be many things: the meander of the mind, the pursuit of a question, the forward-thrust of a life or the agitated, agitating backward glance. For Nicole Chung in *All You Can Ever Know*, the plot revolves around Chung's deep desire to piece together the past she, born of a Korean couple and adopted by a white couple, had not been privy to.

Chung had been listening to the same story all her life. But was it true? "*Your birth parents had just moved here from Korea,*" her parents had told her. "*They thought they wouldn't be able to give you the l life you deserved.*"

Not until Chung is pregnant with her own first child does she begin to do the research and write the letters that will change her understanding of who she is and where she's come from. Not until then will she have the facts she needs to build her own ideas about family, and about belonging. "I know my place in my adoptive family is secure," she says. "That is not the same thing as always feeling that I belong."

THERE WILL BE NO MIRACLES HERE

———

CASEY GERALD

My sense is that literature writ large is trying to help us understand how to live better. When people ask me, Hey my cousin, my nephew, my sister say, I'm thinking about writing a memoir, *I say:* Don't do it. Unless your life depends on it.

That was the case for me. I started this book because I had lived my life into a dead end. I had achieved all these things they tell kids to achieve. But I was very cracked up, as I say very often. Many of my friends were cracked up, too, obviously; this was 2016. So I set out to trace those cracks with words. It turns out the book business is one of the only businesses that will pay you to figure out what is wrong with yourself. And so I started the book, and before I finished, about two or three months into it, one of my closest friends, a little brother friend of mine who had had a similar Horatio Alger journey, except from St. Louis, committed suicide..... I had just gotten into the parts of the book where the narrative expectation is Okay, now you've made it. I got all sad. I couldn't write for a few days. I took a nap, helped with some bourbon, and my friend came to me in a dream. He was sitting in a booth in a diner and he said, You know, Casey. We did a lot of things that we wouldn't advise anyone we love to do. *And then I woke up. It was almost like my friend came from the other side and said,* Here's the book, man. I'll walk with you. I'll help you get there.

The intervention here is to say, Hey, wait a second. Maybe the way we're taught to live is actually killing us. *But I can't just leave it there. I have to try to imagine what it would look like to truly live, to truly be whole, to be free, to be a better person, a better friend, a better lover, to know God for real and not as some senseless ritual. Now how do you get there? That gets to your question around my standard of endurance in literature.*

I got a lot of hell when I first finished this book from people who said, What's with that ending, man? What is this? *I said it was the most honest vision of hope I had at the time. And more importantly—every great story, if you really think about it, has as its end the beginning.... A measure, then, of the stories that will hold up is that there has to be enough in there for mystery.*
— Casey Gerald

Casey Gerald's debut memoir, *There Will Be No Miracles Here*, is, in Gerald's words, an intervention, a confession. It's a tale about the American Dream, and how the American Dream profoundly messes with our heads. Those who follow the Dream's dictates may well crack, Gerald tells us. Those who achieve will have to work extra hard to retreat from the excoriating, lonesome-making pain of winning someone else's idea of a reward. Who gets to say who we get to become? Who gets to suggest that having right now can be as hard as not having was? Who gets to be real in this world, and what are the dangers of trading abiding authenticity for temporary power?

Gerald tells his story in mesmeric fashion. He wants to know what has been wrong with him, because if he can diagnose that, he may just be able to diagnose what is wrong with the rest of us—and lead us toward a more fulfilling, less-grandstanding plan.

Gerald whispers, boldly, of a coming revolution, and we listen because his contraindications, his reverse wisdoms, his reach shatter us reverentially at a time when shatter might just save us.

TOGETHER

JUDY GOLDMAN

My older brother has always called me "the little historian." I'm not only a noticer; I'm also a rememberer. Not surprising then, the starting point for my memoir about my marriage: remembering why we fell in love in the first place. Which led me to a million tiny scenes from the past, all those early snapshots, moments of bliss. But memoir requires that we write about the things that unsettle us, so I needed to also include the times we wondered if we'd made a mistake. My husband is a noticer and rememberer, too. When I began writing this memoir, he and I would be side by side on the sofa, legs outstretched on the ottoman, and I'd ask him, "Name things that happened right after we got married. How 'bout when our daughter was born? When our son left for college and we were alone again?" Marriages are always moving into a new and unfamiliar world where we have never been before. My job as memoirist was to probe the past so that I could record that progression. All the different versions of a marriage.
— Judy Goldman

Once, in a conversation on the PBS show NC Bookwatch, Judy Goldman reflected on a writing career that had begun in poetry, stretched toward fiction, and transitioned into memoir. Memoir, Goldman asserted, was a form of poetry. Memoir was, to her, like returning home. The details of her life would always be her most affixing emotional current.

Together is Goldman's second memoir, after the deeply affecting *Losing My Sister*. It is a book that wonders out loud about what makes a marriage last—after the whirlwind, within the framework of routines, in the aftermath of a shattering error or accident. It is a book about the routine medical procedure that left Goldman's husband in a terrifying paralytic condition—and upended the unspoken rules of a long-time partnership.

I read the book in a single sitting. I called my friend the instant I was done. "Look at what you have achieved," I said, rushing to enumerate. A tenterhook suspense. A tentacled tale. A meditation on what happens to love—over time and all at once. *Together* is a book whose author explores and finally celebrates imperfect love. It is a book that dares to shatter the expected reminisce, pivots on a poem, goes long and short in both sentences and chapters, and builds scenes out of just the right components, which is to say credible dialogue, telling detail, and overriding purpose.

WE KNOW WHEN WE START TO EXAGGERATE.
WE KNOW WHEN WE LIE TO MAKE THINGS FIT
OR TO MAKE THE STORY TURN OUT A CERTAIN,
PERFECTLY SYMMETRICAL, DEEPLY SELF-
CONGRATULATORY WAY. WE KNOW WHEN WHAT
WE WRITE WILL NOT RESONATE WITH THOSE WHO
HAVE LIVED THE ADVENTURE ALONGSIDE US.
WE KNOW WHAT WE ARE DOING.

ACKNOWLEDGMENTS

———

Juncture may be many things—a series of workshops, a newsletter, books, and videos—but what matters most to Bill and me is that Juncture is a place where conversations begin. Many of those who have joined us in McClure, PA, in Cape May, NJ, in Frenchtown, NJ, and at Longwood Gardens and Chanticleer Gardens and the Philadelphia Museum of Art have become our cherished friends. Those who have contributed their stories or recommendations have deepened or challenged our thinking. Those who submitted to our essays contest, *The Walls Between Us*, strengthened our faith in the world beyond. Those who took the time to answer my questions (including, of course, Jacinda Barrett) left me newly curious.

For all who have entered our world through Juncture: thank you. For those who have asked the hard stuff: please keep asking. For those who read or write memoir to find out what matters: you matter. We are grateful.

ABOUT JUNCTURE WORKSHOPS

BETH KEPHART is the award-winning author of 23 books and the 2015/2016 recipient of the Beltran Family Award for Innovative Teaching and Mentoring at the University of Pennsylvania's Kelly Writers House. *Handling the Truth: On the Writing of Memoir* won the 2013 Books for a Better Life Award (Motivational Category) and was named a best writing book by *O Magazine, Poets & Writers*, and many others. *Tell the Truth. Make It Matter.*, a memoir workbook, has been adopted in classrooms nationwide.

Kephart's other books include such novels for young adults as the critically acclaimed *Wild Blues* (Simon & Schuster); *This Is the Story of You* (Chronicle Books), a Junior Library Guild Selection, a 2016 Bank Street winner, and a VOYA Top Ten selection; *One Thing Stolen* (Chronicle Books), a Parents' Choice Gold Medal Selection; *Going Over* (Chronicle Books), a 2014 Booklist Top Ten Historical Fiction for Youth; *Small Damages* (Philomel Books), the 2013 Carolyn W. Field Honor Book; and *Undercover* (Laura Geringer Books/HarperTeen), a five-star book named to numerous Best of the Year lists. Her novels for young adults have been translated into French, Dutch, Brazilian-Portuguese, German, Simplified Chinese, Spanish, and Complex Chinese.

Kephart is a National Book Award finalist (memoir) and a winner of the Speakeasy Poetry Prize. She was awarded grants from National Endowment for the Arts, Pew Fellowship in the Arts, Leeway Foundation, and Pennsylvania Council on the Arts.

Kephart chaired the 2001 National Book Awards Young People's Literature Jury, chaired a PEN First Nonfiction Book jury, judged a *Family Circle* essay contest, and has delivered keynotes and lectures about memoir across the country. She has written for publications ranging from *LitHub, Catapult, Brevity, The Millions, LARB, Ploughshares Blog, Ruminate Blog, Chicago Tribune,* and *New York Times* to *Wall Street Journal, Salon, Philadelphia Inquirer, Shelf Awareness,* and *Publishing Perspectives*. She has led numerous writing workshops in elementary, secondary, university, and community settings. She has twice been featured in large, monthslong installations at the Philadelphia International Airport, was featured on the WHYY-TV show, "The Articulate," and was the June 2016 keynote speaker at the Radnor High commencement ceremony. She is a partner in Juncture Writing Workshops, delivering five-day memoir workshops in selected locales across the country and producing a monthly memoir newsletter.

WILLIAM SULIT is the co-founder of Juncture Workshops. He has collaborated with Beth on multiple book projects as an artist, photographer, and designer. He is an award-winning ceramicist with a master's degree in architecture from Yale University.

Beth and William's first picture book, *Trini's Big Leap* (with Alexander de Wit), is due out in Fall 2019 from Penny Candy, and their second will appear in 2020. They are at work on a series of illustrated journals.

JUNC | TURE

WRITING WORKSHOPS

———

www.junctureworkshops.com

CPSIA information can be obtained
at www.ICGtesting.com
Printed in the USA
LVHW030349301120
673004LV00032B/482

9 781794 607989